ORDINARY HEROES
OF OLD DELMARVA

Also by Jim Duffy/Secrets of the Eastern Shore:

• *Eastern Shore Road Trips #1*
27 One-Day Adventures on Delmarva

• *Tubman Travels*
32 Underground Railroad Journeys on Delmarva

• *Eastern Shore Road Trips #2*
26 MORE One-Day Adventures on Delmarva

• *You Wouldn't Believe*
44 Strange and Wondrous Delmarva Tales

• *Shore Fun!*
The Delmarva Wanderer's Guide

Website
SecretsoftheEasternShore.com

Facebook
Facebook.com/SecretsoftheEasternShore

Bookstores, retail shops, and other purchase options
SecretsoftheEasternShore.com/product-category/books

Feedback
SecretsoftheEasternShore@gmail.com
443.477.4490

ORDINARY HEROES
OF OLD DELMARVA

INSPIRING TRUE TALES OF
COURAGE, KINDNESS, AND COMMUNITY

A Secrets of the Eastern Shore Book
By Jim Duffy

Published by Secrets of the Eastern Shore
Cambridge, Maryland
ISBN: 979-8-9872641-4-0

Cover Design: Jill Jasuta
Interior Design: Paul Clipper

Front cover photo: The mailboat *Handy* arrives at Wharf Creek on Hog Island, Va., 1920. From the collections of the Barrier Islands Center in Machipongo, Va. BarrierIslandsCenter.org

Back cover photos (clockwise from top left): Ruth Starr Rose, John Moaney, Mary Banning, George Hitchens, Dale Wimbrow, Emily Bissell, Robert and Lillie Banks, Thomas Scott.

Feedback
SecretsoftheEasternShore@gmail.com
443.477.4490

More Stories
SecretsoftheEasternShore.com

Ordinary Heroes of Old Delmarva

TABLE OF CONTENTS

Ordinary Heroes of Old Delmarva

INTRODUCTION
PAST FORWARD!

"Elevator speeches" are a challenge for me. Ask what my next book is about and, well, we'd better be in the elevator at the Empire State Building because I'm gonna blab for 100 stories. So it was with this book, until I heard the economist Tyler Cowen say these words on a podcast.

I think there's a future for the past.

Cowen was talking in an academic sense, but I'm going to steal his words and move them onto personal turf. I've spent much of the last decade digging into the history of the Delmarva Peninsula, telling stories about its heroes, its villains, and its everyday folks. It's been the most rewarding stretch of my writing career.

This book was born from a nagging sense of something missing in my storytelling. I'd find a story—ooh, that's interesting! I'd research it. I'd write it. On to the next one!

But readers miss out on something that way. Many of those Delmarva stories didn't fade from my life after I moved on. They had an afterlife, in my heart. Weeks, months, years later, they'd pop into my head, serving like highway signs on the road of life. Oh, that's the direction I should go.

• I'd make a mistake. And that leads to a question: Do I really have to apologize to that jerk? Hmm, WWFDD? What would Frederick Douglass do? See Chapter 19.

• I'd be at a table full of people screaming about politics. I'd squirm in discomfort. Wait, what was it that Chinese laundryman from Cambridge had to say about such moments? There, now I feel better. See Chapter 4.

• Valentine's Day approaches. What sweet thing can I write in my wife's card? Hey, how about that adorable (and oh-so-true) quote about the married life of the lifesaver from Snow Hill? See Chapter 2.

• I'd do a time-consuming favor, but ... c'mon, where's the gratitude? They should have bought me dinner! Did that womanizing snob from Oxford—such an unlikely hero—expect payback from the refugees he saved? See Chapter 7. Did the perfect stranger on the Underground Railroad regret not giving his name and address to Harriet Tubman so she could send him a gift certificate? See Chapter 6.

• I'd feel helpless about this or that big social problem. What can one little person like me do? Tell that to those little schoolgirls from Ridgely. See Chapter 8. Tell that to the otherwise wishy-washy minister who jumped in to help old Sammy down in Accomack County. See Chapter 14.

You get the idea. We're walking on footprints from days gone by when wandering the Delmarva Peninsula. Those footprints are often much more than remnants of a buried past. They point forward, giving guidance for the life ahead.

I think there's a future for the past.

That's the theme. Here's hoping these stories live a long and inspiring afterlife in your heart. Thanks for giving them a shot.

Jim Duffy

1 FRIENDSHIP
THE 'HOUSEBOY' AND THE PRESIDENT

Two men, mid-1900s. One an Army grunt, the other a bigwig general. One a country boy, the other a future president. One black, the other white. One hired as a "houseboy," the other his boss. All friendships are special, but ones that cross seemingly imposing divides can seem especially so. They speak to the way our shared American experiences sometimes ford rivers of class, race, and rank, often with surprising ease.

John Moaney was born in Talbot County on Maryland's Eastern Shore in 1914. It's not clear where, exactly, this blessed event occurred, but John's family roots were deeply entwined in a backroads rural community called Copperville.

That working-class black enclave lies on Miles River Neck, which was home to several plantation-style estates in slavery times. More than 200 slaves toiled at Wye House, owned by the extravagantly rich and powerful Lloyd family.

Frederick Douglass spent childhood time in bondage on that plantation. His family, too, had deep roots in the Miles River Neck area. His beloved grandmother, Betsy Bailey, grew up on land where Copperville would eventually take shape. His rela-

11

tives would remain in the area over many generations to follow—they're still around in Copperville today.

The town that sprung up after the Civil War first took shape with the purchase of small lots by a pair of black veterans of that conflict, Solomon Deshields and John Copper. Early on black folks christened the place with an evocative nickname, the "Village of Liberty."

John Moaney settled into a working-class life as a young adult, taking on jobs in landscaping and as a farmhand. He got married in this window, but alas, his wife died in a car accident. Then, with the winds of war blowing, he enlisted in the Army two months before Pearl Harbor. He landed in a quartermaster unit, doing vehicle maintenance.

Fast forward to summer 1942. A post came open on the staff of an unnamed general. I have no idea how Moaney felt deep down about that job possibility, but the one-word description of its duties—"houseboy"—makes it sound rather distasteful to our modern ears. Nonetheless, Moaney applied. He got the job.

The first indication that maybe he'd landed in a different sort of gig than that description implies came when he met his new boss. Gen. Dwight D. Eisenhower told his new "houseboy" that there would be no saluting and no standing at attention. What he wanted was a man who could make sure that his off-duty hours unfolded without fail in easy, relaxing, and comfortable fashion.

Moaney understood the mission statement this way:

He wanted his "home time" to be like a regular life.

Ike's 'Irreplaceable Man'
It's easy to assume that these two men were very different, one from the other. They occupied different stations in life. They

came from different parts of the country. They had different skin colors—and this was still segregation times to boot.

But that assumption would be wrong. The two men had no trouble finding common ground. The general, too, had humble and mostly rural roots. Eisenhower's father had hit financial rock bottom as one point, after failing in a business venture. One desperate day he put his entire life savings of $24 in his pocket and moved his family to Abilene, Kansas. He got a job as a railroad mechanic. The family got by.

Both men grew up steeped in Christian religion. Eisenhower's mother set aside daily times, after breakfast and after dinner, for family Bible reading sessions. Moaney maintained lifelong ties with the historic Copperville congregation of Deshields United Methodist Church.

Both men had learned in younger years to enjoy hunting and fishing. Both loved farming, too, as well as cooking with fresh, homegrown vegetables. They shared a distaste for fancy chefs and high falutin' cuisine.

As Moaney put it, the general's preferred culinary style was "plain ol' cookin'."

The bond between the grunt and the general was built to last. John Moaney and Dwight Eisenhower would live side by side, day in and day out, morning until night, for most of the next 28 years. They spent World War II together, then the Cold War years in the White House, and then on into Eisenhower's post-presidency retirement.

Asked about Moaney in his later years, here is what Eisenhower had to say:

He and I have been inseparable for more than a quarter of a century. He is just about the irreplaceable man in my life.

13

'I'd Rather Stay By Your Side'
For Dwight D. Eisenhower, "home" was as much an idea as a place. He was often on the move during World War II. He worked out of London for a while, then spent time in North Africa. After D-Day, he lived in tents as American troops marched through France and Germany on the way to victory. In his postwar, pre-presidency years, he lived in Washington, DC, New York City, and Europe.

John Moaney's job during all this moving about was to create a stable, homey refuge for the off-duty Eisenhower. Down-time was precious to the general. It might even qualify as one of the secrets to his success in war and in life. He seems to have had an incredible gift for leaving problems at the office and finding a way amid the comforts of home to step away and recharge.

Moaney told an incredible story about this in an oral his-tory session conducted by Eisenhower historians. In all of those 28 years Moaney spent creating a homey refuge for Eisenhower, there was one and only one time when Moaney sensed his boss was in troubled times. That was in the days before D-Day on June 6, 1944.

At that particular time ... he just was home there in the house, and we had orders not to interfere with him. ... He still had that smile, but I still knew something was wrong.

Moaney stacked his homemaker days one on top of the other. He would start a coal fire in the morning, then make breakfast and so on through one day after another. At the end of the war everyone on Eisenhower's staff was given the chance to return to civilian life. Eisenhower pulled Moaney aside in those days, saying he understood that this was likely the end of the road for their relationship. Moaney had a different idea.

If it's okay with you General, I'd rather stay by your side.

Back stateside Eisenhower landed first in Washington, DC. During this close-to-his-Eastern-Shore-home window Moaney got married for a second time. He'd known Delores Butler in childhood. They shared connections with Deshields church in Copperville. Delores had two daughters from a first marriage.

The Moaneys then followed Eisenhower to New York City when he took a job as president of the Ivy League Columbia University. Then, in 1950, Eisenhower became supreme military commander of the newly formed NATO alliance. That job entailed moving to Europe.

"Well, Moaney," Eisenhower said, "I guess this is the end of the line for us. You'll have to stay here with your new young wife."

Again, Moaney had a different idea.

"General," he replied, "I've known you longer than I've known her. If it's okay by you, I'll stay by your side."

Delores and her daughters moved back to the Washington DC area during the 18 months Eisenhower and Moaney spent in Europe. Then, in 1952, Eisenhower came back to the U.S. to run for president.

Copperville Goes to the White House
After Eisenhower won that election, Moaney joined the White

House staff. There was a crisis on inauguration day in January 1953. That afternoon, after the morning inaugural parade, Moaney learned that Eisenhower's clothes had yet to arrive at the White House. Somehow, the movers had left those particular bags behind at a train station. Eisenhower could tell by Moaney's expression that there was a problem.

"What's the matter, Moaney?"
"I can't find your clothes to wear to the ball tonight."
"I'm glad you can't find them! I won't have to go!"

Moaney managed to find those clothes in time, and poor Eisenhower had to endure that inauguration ball.

These White House years are when Delores Moaney enters the Eisenhower picture in a fuller way. She, too, joined the White House staff. As time unfolded, she even became the subject of a running joke among the White House press corps, who laughed publicly on several occasions about how frequently the Eisenhowers gave nights off to their fancy White House chef and his staff. They did that so that Delores could have the run of the kitchen, as she apparently had mastered the art of "plain ol' cookin'" while growing up in the Talbot County countryside.

Eisenhower cherished his downtime as much in the presidency as he had in war time. Fishing and golfing were his two favorite escapes. He and Moaney spent countless idle hours in small boats, just the two of them floating on this lake or along that river. Moaney's responsibilities as a caddy on the links led to another recurring joke among the White House press corps. This one had Ike lining up to take a shot and Moaney wandering up the fairway or onto the green in anticipation of what was about to happen. Almost invariably, the jokes went, Moaney would stop at a spot and Eisenhower's shot would come to rest nearly at his feet.

Moaney traveled quite a bit across America with Eisenhower during the segregation years of the late 1940s and early 1950s. Every time the famous general and later, president, learned that a hotel or restaurant said they wouldn't serve blacks, Eisenhower would inform them that well, in that case he wouldn't be dining or staying with them.

Invariably, the business owners changed their tune and bent their rules.

Most of the time during this long window Moaney worked seven days a week. He was about his tasks before Eisenhower awoke (usually, 7am). He wrapped things up only after Eisenhower went to sleep. The Eisenhower historians who conducted that oral-history interview were flabbergasted by this, but Moaney brushed their disbelief aside in two short comments.

I never felt right going to bed until he come in and go to bed.

I never bothered with a day off. I was mostly just satisfied.

The biggest day for the Delmarva Peninsula in all of this came on June 11, 1957. That was the day the Eisenhowers invited a group from Deshields United Methodist Church to visit the White House. Some 40 folks from Copperville enjoyed that honor, including John Moaney's mother. The official photo of that event is a glorious affair, full of broad smiles and now-vintage fashions.

A National Park Service account of the friendship between Eisenhower and Moaney includes a charming anecdote about this day. Apparently, just before the photo was snapped, the president and his wife, Mamie, had to call out first to John and then to Delores to demand that they move from obscure hiding places in the back into positions of prominence.

One Last Home Sweet Home: Gettysburg

You might guess that the day Copperville visited the White House would rank as John and Delores Moaney's favorite memory of their Eisenhower years, but you'd be wrong. The oral-history session those Eisenhower historians conducted with Moaney happened in the Gettysburg, Pa. home where the Eisenhowers lived in retirement after the presidency.

Today, that home is the Eisenhower National Historic Site. If you visit you'll find the bedroom used by the Moaneys re-created exactly as it was in the 1960s. Docents there will tell you all about the beautiful friendship between the Moaneys and the Eisenhowers.

This house, then, is where Moaney was sitting when asked to pick the very best time in his career at Eisenhower's side. He didn't talk about the Allies winning World War II. He didn't mention the presidency or the glamor of the White House. He just had two words to say.

Right here.

It was those quieter retirement years that he cherished most. In an interview in her later years, Delores put a similar thought in even blunter terms.

I couldn't wait to get away from that White House. It just wasn't a place to attract my attention.

Dwight Eisenhower died in the late 1960s. John Moaney died in the late 1970s. Eisenhower's widow, Mamie, was among a large contingent of Eisenhowers who made a pilgrimage to Copperville to console Delores and attend John's funeral at Deshields Methodist.

Delores lived to the ripe old age of 98. She retained close ties with the Eisenhower family all the way to the end. Several sweet photos on the internet show an elderly Delores holding this or that Eisenhower grandchild. She died in 2017.

The friendship between Dwight Eisenhower and John Moaney rates as a little footnote in American history. But it's a footnote worth pondering, isn't it? A lovely reminder that the much-discussed divides of culture, class, and race often prove paper-thin—and nothing to be scared of. It's a reminder, too, that the work of bridging such divides unfolds in one-on-one fashion with neighbors, co-workers, and passing acquaintances. We might never hit that Moaney/Eisenhower jackpot of becoming "irreplaceable" to each other, but smaller triumphs count, too, in the hunt for shared, common ground.

2 COURAGE
THOMAS SCOTT LEAPS ABOARD A SINKING SHIP

Imagine it's December of 1869. You are aboard an early-morning ferry crossing from New Jersey to New York City. You are chilled to the bone—yet again! New York has been in the grips of an icy cold spell for several weeks now. Day after day, a wicked northwest wind blows.

There is ice on the Hudson River, but that's no cause for concern. Just like on every other day of the deep freeze, the ferry chugs its way along, big paddle wheels crunching through the frozen mess, no problem. Hundreds of passengers are aboard, quite a few women with young children among them.

Then, trouble. The ferry slows. The paddle wheels struggle. The whole vessel creaks to a halt. Is the ice just too thick? Did the pilot make some stupid mistake? Some passengers groan in frustration, realizing that they're going to be late for work or meetings or medical appointments.

Nearby is a tugboat, cruising along innocently. The tug thwacks into a hunk of ice so big that it knocks the tug off course. Suddenly, that tug is headed directly for your ferry …

KA-THUNK!

No detailed accounts of the first moments of this near disaster survive. Quite possibly, the impact knocks you and some fellow passengers off balance. Did gasps of fright fill the air? Did one of those babies skitter from a mother's grasp?

The tug reverses engines, backing off. And now shock turns into terror. At the waterline of your ferry is a V-shaped gash. The icy waters of the Hudson are rushing right through. Moments later, the ferry lurches over, listing badly over to the side where that gaping hole keeps sucking in water.

Shrieks went up from hundreds of throats. Women, with blanched faces, caught terror-stricken children in their arms, while men, crazed with fear, scaled the rails and upper decks to escape the plunging of the overthrown horses.

How many minutes do you and your fellow passengers have left in life—two, five, fifteen? Is there anything that can stop the Hudson from claiming this ferry and dragging her down into the icy depths?

Another tug approaches, this one called the *Reliance*. She belongs to a marine salvage company. On her deck, surveying the accident scene, stands a man who grew up sailing the waters of the Eastern Shore. Captain Thomas Albertson Scott is a native of Snow Hill, Md.

What Makes a Hero?
A brief diversion to the faraway land of Mongolia. In *The Mongol Queens*, historian Jack Weatherford relays a story from the time of Genghis Khan in which Altani, a girl of around 12 years old,

saved the life of a 4-year-old boy by making a series of split-second decisions. She sprinted after the full-grown guy who had kidnapped the boy, then leapt on his back and corralled his arm in a way that kept him from stabbing the boy. A minute or two later some soldiers showed up to help Altani save the day. That boy was one of Genghis Khan's sons.

In the Mongol perspective, challenges choose us, but we choose how to respond. Destiny brings the opportunities and the misfortunes, and the merit of our lives derives from those unplanned moments.

The Mongols ... placed great importance on sudden individual acts of unexpected heroism. Those are the moments that reveal not just the character of the person, but the soul itself. Many people are paralyzed by fear or, equally as debilitating, by indecision. The hero acts, and often fails, but acts nonetheless.

Such a person belongs to the spiritual elite of the divinely blessed and heavenly inspired baatar, a person filled with a firm, strong, unyielding spirit. Usually translated simply as "hero," the word is much more important in Mongolian, containing an emphasis on the personal will behind the act [and the way] the hero ... acts immediately and decisively without concern for personal benefit or even survival.

Unlike the Greek heroes, who were males of superhuman physical strength, the baatar might be male or female, young or old, and frequently, as in this case, only a child. Most important, a baatar might spring from any family, but, in Genghis Khan's experience, the baatuud rarely came from rich families or aristocratic and powerful clans. He placed such importance on the spirit of the baatuud that he built his military and political system around them. The ideal government for him was rule by these heroic elites, by a true aristocracy of the spirit.

The Search for Family Roots
If Captain Thomas Scott had lived in Mongol empire times, he would have landed at the top of that heroic aristocracy. A history buff named Vaughn Baker tipped me off to Scott's story. A former chair of the board at the Edward H. Nabb Research Center for Delmarva History and Culture, he got interested in Thomas Scott while researching an ancestor named Captain Jimmy Scott, who lived on Assateague Island.

Family legend said Jimmy had a brother who moved up around New York City and became an early undersea diver while working on building lighthouses and bridges. Back in the 1980s Baker was traveling north of New York City when he stumbled upon a historic marker about a diver named Thomas Scott. Back home, he did some more digging but came up empty.

Fast forward 30 years. Baker is in the New York area again. He wants to find that historic marker but can't remember where it was. After giving up, Baker ends up in the waterfront area of New London, Connecticut, where, much to his surprise, he comes upon a restaurant called the Captain Thomas Scott Lobster Dock. On the wall is a portrait of Thomas Scott. Its caption refers to a "legend" that he was born in Maryland. It cites various marine construction and salvage projects that earned him a measure of fame during his lifetime. It mentions an old biography.

The game is afoot once more.

Not Bad for a Lad from Snow Hill
After getting that tip from Mr. Baker, I took a turn jumping down that rabbit hole. There is a century-old biography, *Captain Thomas Scott, Master Diver: One Who Was Not Afraid and Who Spoke*

the Truth. The author is another Maryland native, Baltimore-born Francis Hopkinson Smith. Smith's first career was in marine engineering. He was in charge of laying the foundation for the Statue of Liberty.

Later in life Smith became quite a popular writer. His bestselling novel *Caleb West* has a hero modeled after Captain Scott. That novel became a Broadway play, and that play became a Hollywood movie in the silent era. That's a pretty impressive run of attention paid by the big wide world to a lad from Snow Hill with little schooling. By all indications Thomas Scott got the bulk of his education working the water. He was captain of a little pungy at the tender age of 15.

Smith had gotten to know Captain Scott during his time as a marine engineer. Their first project together was Race Rock Lighthouse in Long Island Sound. Race Rock is recognized today as a grand feat of engineering for its time. Laying the sprawling underwater foundation of masonry took seven long years.

Shortly after Smith agreed to sign on as the engineer who would get that lighthouse built, he realized that the job was beyond his capabilities. He describes himself as "young [and] inexperienced, with little money and with practically no plan." But the desperation he felt about that project disappeared in an instant when Captain Thomas Scott walked into his office for a job interview. Have you ever met someone like that, who washed away your worries in an instant, by just showing up and carrying themselves in a certain way?

No man or child could look Captain Thomas A. Scott in the face without instantly believing in him, and no act of his [later in] life would shake that belief.

24

Smith's admiration for Scott grew from there. While working side by side with the Worcester County native through that Race Rock Lighthouse project, Smith learned a little bit about Captain Scott's background.

In 1866, there sailed out of a harbor on the Chesapeake, near the town of Snow Hill, Maryland, a craft carrying eight cords of wood all on deck. She was what was known as a "bay pungy," drawing but four feet of water, with a mast forward and a boom swinging loose. The captain was Tommy Scott, a lad of fifteen— strong, well-built, and springy, with a look in his face of one who was not afraid, and who spoke the truth. The crew was a negro boy of twelve. These two supplied neighboring towns with wood in exchange for oysters and clams.

Some years later a straight, clear-eyed young fellow, with a chest of iron, arms like cant hooks, and thighs lashed with whip-cord and steel, shipped as a common sailor aboard the schooner John Willetts. ... He was seven years older than when he commanded the pungy, but the look on his face was still the same—the look of a man who was not afraid and who spoke the truth.

Young Thomas Scott quickly climbed the ranks of the wider maritime world. Three years later he was captain of his own schooner, the *Thomas Nelson*. During one hair-raising return trip from Barbados, illness took the life of his navigator and left the rest of his crew bedridden. Without that navigator Scott had only the vaguest of notions where he was headed. A storm for the ages rolled through. The only healthy helper available was his inexperienced wife.

The Atlantic was an unknown sea to Scott, but the wife and all he had in the world was aboard. Forty-eight hours the two stood on deck taking turns at the pumps and tiller. ...

They survived the storm. Their journey back to land without a navigator took 25 days.

[The Thomas Nelson] dropped anchor in the Roanoke [at last]. Many a storm have these two ridden out together since that blind rush from ... Barbados. Storms of poverty, of death, of sorrow— many a bright morning too, and welcoming harbor, have gladdened their eyes, but there were always four hands on the tiller, two big and strong and two warm and helping.

Jumping Aboard that Sinking Ferry

The couple ended up in the Coytesville neighborhood of Fort Lee, New Jersey. Scott walked away from the water briefly to open a general store, but returned soon enough to maritime life. He tackled a mix of salvage and construction jobs. He was working one such gig during that bone-chilling spell of 1869 when he spied that ferry in distress.

Like a Mongol *baatar*, Scott ordered his *Reliance* to pull alongside the ferry. The scene on board was pandemonium. No one knew what to do. Passengers and crew were sprinting to and fro in panicked disarray. I am going to let Smith tell most of the story that follows, since he does such a great job of it.

[Captain Scott] sprang forward, stooped down, ran his eye along the water-line, noted in a flash every shattered plank, climbed into the pilot-house of his own boat, and before the astonished pilot could catch his breath ran the nose of the Reliance along the rail

of the ferry-boat and dropped upon the latter's deck like a cat. If he had fallen from a passing cloud the effect could not have been more startling. Men crowded about him and caught his hands. Women sank on their knees and hugged their children, and a sudden peace and stillness possessed every soul on board.

Scott spied a man who had snatched a life-preserver and was now clinging to it. He decided that this was the moment to send a message to everyone about staying calm, and about looking out first for the women and children.

Tearing [the] life-preserver from the man ... and throwing it overboard, he backed the coward ahead of him through the swaying mob, ordering the people to stand clear, and forcing the whole mass [of passengers] to the starboard side. The increased weight gradually righted the stricken boat until she regained a nearly even keel.

With a threat to throw overboard any man who stirred, he dropped into the engine-room, met the engineer [who was] halfway up the ladder [and trying to escape.] [Scott] compelled him to return, [then started to drag] mattresses from the crew's bunks [and strip] off blankets, racks of clothes, overalls, cotton waste, and rags of carpet, cramming them into the great rent [in the side of the ferry], until the space of each broken plank was replaced, except one. Through and over this space the water still [flowed in], deluging the floors and swashing down between the gratings into the hold below.

"'Another mattress!" he cried, "Quick!" But there were no more mattresses.

"All gone? A blanket then—carpet—anything! Five minutes more and she'll right herself. Quick, for God's sake!"

It was useless. Everything, even to the oil rags, had been used. "Your coat, then. Think of the babies, man; do you hear them?" Coats and vests were off in an instant; the engineer on his knees bracing the shattered planking, Captain Scott forcing the garments into the splintered openings. It was useless. Little by little the water gained, bursting out first below, then [over on] one side, ... [rushing] in again.

Captain Scott stood a moment as if undecided, ran his eye searchingly over the engine-room, saw that for his needs it was empty, then deliberately tore down the top wall of caulking he had so carefully built up, and, before the engineer could protest, ... forced his own body into the gap with his arm outside level with the drifting ice.

An hour later the disabled ferryboat, with every soul on board [alive], was towed into the Hoboken slip. When they lifted the captain from the wreck he was unconscious and barely alive. The water had frozen his blood, and the floating ice had torn the flesh from his protruding arm from shoulder to wrist.

When the color began to creep back to his cheeks, he opened his eyes, and said to the doctor who was winding the bandages: "Wuz any of them babies hurt?"

From a *New York Herald* newspaper story on the rescue:

This is the first record of a leak of this size being stopped by a man's body at the risk of his own life. Possibly several hundred lives were saved by the bravery of Captain Scott.

'Cursing Like a Pirate'
A month passed before Captain Thomas Scott regained a measure of his earlier health and strength. He returned to his work on the

Reliance, but soon departed that job in anger. As things turned out, the powers that be at his salvage company decided to send a bill to the ferry company, demanding payment for the heroics of its employee.

This bill soon became the subject of dispute, with the parties involved landing in court. Captain Scott got called into the office of the president of the salvage company.

"Captain," said the official, "we're going to have some trouble getting our pay for that ferry job. Here's an affidavit for you to swear to."

[Captain Scott] took the paper to the window and read it through without a comment, then laid it back on the president's desk, picked up his hat, and moved to the door.

"Did you sign it?"

"No! I ain't a-goin' to."

"Why?"

"[Be]cause I ain't so durned mean as you be. Look at this [injured] arm [of mine]. Do you think I [would have gone] into that hellhole if it hadn't been for them women cryin' and the babies a-hollerin'? And you want 'em to pay for it? Damn ye!"

Then he walked out, cursing like a pirate.

Soon thereafter an unemployed Captain Thomas Scott showed up in the office of Francis Hopkinson Smith, responding to an ad seeking someone to take charge of the dangerous construction work ahead at the proposed Race Rock Lighthouse. Smith adds one last fun tidbit to this story. Years later, he reports, Scott dug out from an old trunk the ship's log of the *Reliance*. He shared with Smith its comically brief summary of the events of that icy day on the Hudson River:

Left Jersey City 7 a.m. Ice running heavy. Captain Scott stopped leak in ferry-boat.

Captain Thomas Scott was 42 years old on the day of these hero-ics. He lived a long and rather storied life after that, starting his own marine salvage company and winning a good bit of renown for his ability to clear shipwrecks and rescue cargo where other companies had failed. The biography of him that Smith wrote came out in 1908, the year after Captain Thomas Albertson Scott had died at the age of 77. Here is how that book ends:

... in the thirty-seven years I knew and loved him, he has always been, and will always be, to those who had his confidence, one of nature's noblemen – brave, modest capable, and tenderhearted. The record of his life must be of value to his fellow countrymen. Nor can I think of any other higher tribute to pay him than to repeat the refrain... one who was not afraid and spoke the truth, a description of Tommy Scott even at age 15.

3 TRUE GRIT
ELIZABETH FULTON PLAYS SUPERHERO IN THE STORM OF 1936

Put your 18-year-old shoes on. Remember those days?

Sorry. This is not going to be a carefree exercise. Once you're laced up, step straight out into the teeth of a Category 3 hurricane. You're on a beach, alongside your husband—yes, you married quite young in this alternate life. The fishing cabin you were renting just got swept out to sea. You're six miles from help. A monstrous wave soars over top of you. Wait, where's your husband? There he is, screaming and flailing.

That wave is pulling him out into the furious sea.

Have you read any young-adult fantasy novels? Whaddya think? Could your 18-year-old self have summoned up the mix of courage, pluck, strength, and smarts displayed by the teenage-girl heroes of those books?

Elizabeth Fulton rose to that challenge in heroic fashion along the beaches of Assateague Island back in 1936. We'll get to her story soon enough. First, some scene setting.

31

A Hard Rain's Supposed to Fall
Back in September 2024 I had planned to spend a week wandering around the Smoky Mountains, chasing Cherokee footsteps. Just as my trip began, however, Hurricane Helene showed up in weather forecasts. It was the heavy rain in those forecasts that led me to cut that trip short and head home.

I had no idea what was really coming—hundreds of deaths, thousands of homes destroyed, scores of billions in economic losses. Like everyone else in those days, I prayed for miracles while following the news, longing for tales of survival and rescue to pop up amid the tragedies.

Something clicked in my brain—another storm, long ago. The Mid-Atlantic Hurricane of 1936 isn't a famous Delmarva storm, but maybe it deserves more attention. The aftermath of that storm served up more than its share of those little miracles we long for when natural disasters strike.

Mother Nature made the first miraculous turn. Experts thought the storm would make a devastating direct hit on Delmarva, as the Category 3 monstrosity was barreling straight as an arrow toward landfall on the Outer Banks of North Carolina. But then it made a surprise turn, rounding as if along the crook of a shepherd's staff to head back out to sea.

Inland Delmarva was spared. But the outer edges of the storm landed a wicked blow on the Maryland coast. It piled 12 inches of sand atop some of the streets in Ocean City. Chunks of that town's famous oceanfront boardwalk ended up on Baltimore Avenue.

Assateague Island got the worst of the wind, waves, and storm surge. The island wasn't a national seashore yet. It was dotted in those days with vacation cabins popular with anglers. The storm swept a dozen of those cabins out to sea, mostly on remote lower Assateague, some 20 miles below Ocean City, near the Virginia border.

Up in Delaware the danger zone was just offshore. Vessels that didn't make it into the protected waters behind the Delaware Breakwater in time found themselves in deep trouble.

The newspaper headlines the next day were horrific. Maryland:

Sixteen people assumed dead

The Delaware number was even bigger:

42 Men Unreported

These were mostly African American workers aboard the *Long Island*, a commercial fishing vessel out of Lewes. Returning from a week of working off the coast of New Jersey, they had no idea the storm was coming. The boat went down fast.

Just three survivors from the *Long Island* made it ashore that first day. All three had hung onto floating wreckage, riding the waves back to shore. Richard McQuillen was the first to land on the beach. So exhausted he could barely speak, he gave the Coast Guard this bottom line:

The Long Island *down. Crew lost.*

The other two men who landed on the beach looked "like strange dead men [walking] out of the churning ocean." They'd been riding storm-tossed waves for seven hours. One of them told the Coast Guard:

*We saw [our fishing vessel] capsize and [we] saw the other fel-
lows go down. They called for help but we couldn't do a thing.*

The Coast Guard took those reports as gospel. They commenced
looking for bodies, not survivors.

Dead Men, Savoring a 'Hearty Breakfast'

So that's 16 dead on Assateague and 42 offshore of Lewes, a total
of 58. Then came the miracles: Over the next two days, the deaths
of 48 of those 58 people would prove to be greatly exaggerated.

     Start with those fishermen. The news of those 42 deaths
seemed real for 30 long hours—the poor families of those crew
members! Then a Coast Guard vessel on post-storm patrol
checked in on a big coal barge anchored inside the breakwater.
On board were 32 of those 42 "dead" men, all alive and well. Not
only that:

[They were] eating a hearty breakfast.

The three survivors misread what happened—understandably
so, considering they'd been clinging desperately to wreckage
and watching events unfold at a distance obscured by hurricane
winds, waves, and rain.

     What those survivors didn't see was a magnificent bit of
seamanship. Under the guidance of Capt. William M. Bertrand of
Lewes—he'd been through a wreck like this once before—crew
members somehow managed to secure and launch one of the
small boats they used to set seine nets. They managed to get 32
men aboard. Then they sailed through the teeth of the storm into
the breakwater, where they pulled up to the coal barge and asked
for refuge.

Burial Right: How Elizabeth Fulton Saved Her Husband
The news was even better on Assateague Island. There, all 16
people reported as dead survived. Some of these victims managed
to flee before the storm swept their cabins away and then trudge
through miles of wind and rain to reach the closest Coast Guard
station, at Green Run.

Others had a rougher ride. Thomas Robinson got swept
out to sea with his cabin, but he grabbed onto some debris and
rode the waves until they pushed him ashore. Several other survivors had similar ordeals.

Then there is 18-year-old Elizabeth Fulton. That young
woman from Salisbury, Md. stepped into the role of hero with an
incredible display of bravery, strength, and ingenuity. It's unclear
how, exactly, she and her 23-year-old husband, E.R. Fulton, managed to get out of their cabin before it was swept to sea, but they
did.

The couple set out on foot along the beach, storm raging.
The Green Run Coast Guard station was six long miles away.
Disaster struck. Mr. Fulton got scooped up by a surprise mountain
of a wave and dragged out toward the ocean.

Mrs. Fulton sprinted into the violent surf. After a struggle
the teenager managed to drag her husband's wet body back onto
the beach. But the situation remained precarious. Mr. Fulton was
injured. Worse, he'd lost his mind. Did he suffer a head injury?
Did anxiety morph into all-out panic? No telling. What we know
from old newspaper articles is that he was delirious, screaming all
kinds of stuff that didn't make any sense.

Somehow, Elizabeth Fulton came up with an ingenious
plan. She piled sand on top of his body, then piled some more—
and some more, so much sand that Mr. Fulton was completely

buried except for the mouth and face he needed to keep breathing.

The stories that ran about this incident don't give Mrs. Fulton a chance to explain her thinking, but here's my speculation:

• Burying him like that made it less likely he'd get swept away by another wave.

• Second, it kept the rain and wind at bay, giving him a chance to calm down and regain his senses.

• Third, the sand protected him from any dangerous debris carried in by waves or blown around by wind.

Did I mention that Elizabeth Fulton was just 18 years old?

She sat by his side for hours, waiting for the weather to clear a bit. When it did, Mr. Fulton was still in iffy shape, but improved. She scooped and brushed that sand off of him. Then, half carrying her husband and half dragging him, she set out along the beach. Thank God she didn't have to do that for six miles. A pair of patrolling Coast Guardsmen found the couple and helped them make it the rest of the way.

Both Fultons survived. One newspaper report said that the moment Mrs. Fulton crossed the threshold, setting foot in the Coast Guard station, she collapsed in a heap. She wasn't injured, just completely spent, emotionally and physically. Two days passed before she recovered enough to go home.

I went looking in old newspapers to try and figure out what became of the Fultons, hoping that they shared a long, happy life together. Alas, I came up empty in that search. All I've got from the life of Elizabeth Fulton is this one night of crisis when a teenager summoned up incredible reserves of strength and bravery and ingenuity.

I started this chapter talking about miracles. That word implies divine intervention, but this young woman made her own miracle. If I ever write a young adult fantasy novel, I think I know what name I'll give to the heroine.

4 COMMUNITY
THE CHINESE LAUNDRYMAN AS TOAST OF THE TOWN

Judging by their last names, the men who clambered into a "large touring car" and left Cambridge, Md. on a Wednesday in late May of 1910 represented the upper crust of Dorchester County society. There is a Mount Rushmore aspect to their surnames—Brannock, Hopkins, Hearn, and Willey. For centuries those families have loomed large in local lore and civic leadership.

But I mention this car ride not in the context of Cambridge high society—or at least, not yet. What we are talking about here is a duckpin bowling team. Those four men were headed down the road to Salisbury as an all-star outfit representing Cambridge in a five-game match against that town's "strong duckpin team."

Reading the local newspaper story about this expedition from the vantage point of more than a century down the road, what leaps out is the name of the fifth member of Cambridge's duckpin aristocracy: Lee Fong. How in the world did a Chinese immigrant end up in that car with a Brannock, a Hopkins, a Hearn, and a Willey?

The answer to that question lies in an unlikely civic love

story between a Delmarva town and its Chinese laundryman.

Unwelcome Arrivals: The Big Picture of Chinese Immigration

In the years after the Civil War Chinese laborers came to America's West Coast in large numbers. Many toiled on the Transcontinental Railroad. Others chased one or another of the gold rush frenzies that erupted in those decades. Still others opened small businesses or took low-wage jobs.

Too many Americans treated these new neighbors like dirt. Chinese immigrants were victims of unfair discrimination and unjust law enforcement. They often endured unprovoked violence. A vicious public outcry arose over their presence, marred by frequent talk about the threat they posed to "racial purity."

Chinese immigrants were relegated to second-class legal status. They were ineligible for citizenship. They were barred from testifying in court. Then, in 1882, the U.S. Congress passed the Chinese Exclusion Act barring immigration from China for 10 years. That would eventually turn into 50 years, as the restrictions were extended over and over again, all the way into the 1930s.

During much of this period Chinese immigrants were required to carry at all times a "certificate of residence" issued by the Internal Revenue Service. Without proper papers they could be deported in short order.

On Delmarva: Few and Far Between

Lee Fong arrived in North America in the midst of this ugliness. According to a sketchy summary of his life that appeared in a 1916 article in the Cambridge *Banner*, he arrived in 1888. He was 18 years old. He landed first in Ottawa, Canada, then moved to Boston in 1892. It's not clear how, exactly, he got around those 1888 legal obstacles. Was he allowed in because he came through

Canada, rather than directly from China? Was there some loophole he qualified for? We don't know.

What we do know is that his stay in Boston was brief, and it was followed by short stays in Connecticut, Washington, D.C., and Baltimore. Then, in 1895, Fong found his way across the Chesapeake Bay to the Eastern Shore, landing in Cambridge. Searchable databases for the Cambridge *Banner* newspaper don't begin until 1907, so Lee Fong's first dozen or so years in town are mostly a blank slate. The 1900 census lists him as 30 years old and a laundryman.

That career choice is no surprise. Excluded from many traditional jobs, Chinese immigrants often had no choice but to start businesses—most frequently laundries, restaurants, or grocery stores. The laundry game had dirt cheap overhead in pre-electricity days—basically, soap, scrub boards, irons, and ironing boards. Plus, laundries could operate in pretty much any old building, including ramshackle ones with dirt-cheap rents.

To say that Chinese immigrants were few and far between in Maryland in those years is an understatement The 1870 census listed a grand total of two Chinese people in the whole state. By 1900 that number had climbed to 544 individuals. But the bulk of them lived in Baltimore City. Just 189 Chinese immigrants lived in the rest of the state, about eight per county.

A few years back the Delmar Historical and Art Society looked into how many such immigrants were on the Delmarva Peninsula. They found Chinese laundries in the 1900 census in at least 10 towns—Laurel, Milton, and Lewes, Del.; Chincoteague and Onancock, Va.; and Salisbury, Snow Hill, Berlin, Crisfield, and, of course, Cambridge Md. Here is more from that article:

The few [Chinese immigrants] that were here in the late 1800s and early 1900s were almost all owners and operators of laundries. ... They would eke out a living working 18-hour days, 6 days a week, closing only on Sunday due to community pressure. Usually single and in their 30s [these men] had no social outlets and would usually move after a few years.

An Exception to the Lonely Laundryman Rule

That description doesn't fit Lee Fong. He stayed in Cambridge for decades. During that time he somehow climbed the social ladder and became a much-beloved local business owner and civic leader. You can catch hints of this now and again in the local paper. There is his name, in a list of citizens buying war bonds. There it is again, making a large donation in support of the hospital. A full list of Lee Fong's civic do-gooder donations would stretch on for quite a while.

His Star Laundry facility was located on Poplar Street, a one-block-and-done stretch of downtown Cambridge. The business was successful enough that he placed prominent paid ads in nearly every issue of the local paper. In 1913 the *Banner* reported that Fong was making a major new investment in his business.

Lee Fong, the well-known proprietor of the Star Laundry, has recently installed a number of pieces of machinery which are run by electricity; in fact Lee states that his whole plant is now electrified. The different machines have attracted much attention during the past few days.

But Lee Fong's success in Cambridge was more than a matter of business acumen and charitable donations. There was his prowess as a duckpin bowling all-star, for example. He was apparently just as talented in traditional tenpin bowling. In March 1909 the *Ban-*

ner reported that while a team of Cambridge All-Stars had lost a match to a team of Baltimore All-Stars, Lee Fong had performed so brilliantly in defeat that he was invited to return to Baltimore and give an instructional demonstration to bowlers in the big city.

Fong was an avid horseman as well. Here is a public notice he published in the *Banner* in 1913:

I hereby challenge any horse in Dorchester County to run with my horse, 'Star' [on] July 4th. I will give two dozen Chinese dishes to any horse that can beat my horse on the above-named date. This race to be mile heats, three best in five.

Then there was his biggest love, baseball. That sport had spread like wildfire around the country in the late 1800s. The Delmarva Peninsula didn't have a formal league operating in the early 1900s, but pretty much every town fielded a team that would travel around the peninsula playing against other towns.

In 1907 the man chosen to lead a traditional opening-day parade through the streets of downtown and then over to the ballpark was ... our Chinese laundryman. According to the Society for American Baseball Research (SABR), Fong "was one of the primary financial backers of Cambridge baseball during these years and considered the [team's] 'star rooter.'" One player on the Cambridge team that year was future baseball Hall of Famer Frank "Home Run" Baker, a native of nearby Trappe.

On occasion during these years the Chinese laundryman would put together his own team. He sometimes dubbed them "Lee Fong's All-Stars." Fans would come out to watch the All-Stars play exhibition games against teams from other Delmarva towns, barnstorming teams from out of state, and even the local high school team. The Cambridge *Banner*, 1911:

42

Lee Fong, the well-known all-around sporting man, has requested us to say that he challenges the Cambridge High School base-ball team to play a nine-inning game ... on June 5 ... at the new Athletic Park.

The day after that game:

[Lee Fong's] Pick-Up baseball team defeated the Cambridge High School team yesterday afternoon in one of the best played games of the season. The game was an unusually close one, and the interest of the spectators was keyed up to the highest pitch all through the contest.

Two more names from Cambridge's historical upper crust made an appearance in that story. The last name of the guy who pitched for Fong's team was Applegarth. Behind the plate at catcher was a member of the Phillips clan.

'The Best Place in the World'
In 1916 Fong made an announcement that shocked and saddened his adopted community. He planned to sell the Star Laundry and move away from Cambridge. As those plans came to fruition and Fong departed, the *Banner* published a lengthy farewell that's not just fond, but downright fawning. Here are excerpts:

There are comparatively few persons in Cambridge who do not know Lee Fong; old and young, rich and poor, high and low, all classes, kinds, and conditions of people were on good terms with the friendly laundryman from the celestial kingdom. Lee was an all-around sport and good fellow.

He loved baseball, and his was usually the first money that was put up to secure a team, and his $5 was the first to be offered as a reward for a home run knocked out by a member of the Cambridge team; he was an enthusiastic duckpin and tenpin roller; he loved a good horse, and, in time, learned to like the automobile: he was also an ardent bicyclist several years ago, when the craze existed, and he even fell for a good game of pool.

The story then details some of Fong's bowling exploits, along with a rumor that he had been offered a considerable sum of money by a Philadelphia sponsor to go on a bowling tour and put on exhibitions in cities around the country.

Lee modestly declined, saying that he was at home in Cambridge, and knew everybody and everybody knew him, but that it would be different at other places.

By his good nature, his honesty, his liberality, and his earnest efforts to please, Lee Fong made a host of friends in Cambridge, and when a short time ago he announced that he had sold his business and was going back to China, there was a feeling of genuine regret upon the part of these many friends.

This is where the newspaper provided that brief overview of his journey from China to Canada to Boston and, eventually, to the Delmarva Peninsula.

Since [1895] he has been a resident of Cambridge, and during all of the twenty-one years spent in the midst of, at first, a strange people, he conducted himself in such a way as to win the confidence and esteem of the general public. He was an enthusiast in everything but politics; about politics, he said he did not know anything, only he wanted to see his friends win and was always willing to help them.

The story says that Fong had a brother in New York City and a son back in China who was now a young adult. Apparently, Fong had been trying for years to bring that son to America, but he hadn't managed to get that done in the face of those anti-Chinese immigration rules. The story continues:

When asked what he would do in China, Lee Fong stated that he would not do anything: that a little American money would go a long way in China, and that he expected to carry enough with him to last him for several months, during which time he would visit his family and other relatives.

His many friends here wish the genial Chinaman the best kind of a trip, all kinds of luck, and safe trip to and from the celestial empire ... [We] hope to see his smiling countenance in Cambridge before very many moons have rolled around. This [would] not be at all surprising, as Lee stated just before he left that Cambridge was the best place in the world to him and that he would surely come back.

Fong was a man of his word. He returned to Cambridge in 1918 and opened another laundry in a different building on Poplar Street. Again his name starts popping up in ads and occasional news stories and public notices in the local paper. He issued a plea in December of 1918 asking whoever took "a large clothes basket" to please return it. In 1922 he offered a reward of $25 for information about the delinquents who broke a window at his business, then came inside to play craps and poker. That same year Lee Fong made another nice donation to the local "hospital fund."

Searchable access to the Cambridge newspaper runs out after 1922, so it's hard to track what happened to Lee Fong in his later years. My friend Cheryl Hannan, who (unlike me) knows her way around genealogy sites, found Fong in the 1930 census operating his business at 15 Poplar Street and living with a 24-year-old son, Wong. The census says Wong arrived in 1925.

Things take a turn in the 1940 census. Lee Fong is not listed on Poplar Street. Instead, the laundry is listed as being operated by 33-year-old "James Wong." That age matches up pretty well with that of the younger Fong from a decade before. My guess is that Lee Fong's son adopted an Americanized name. Newspaper reports in 1946 indicate that James Wong got into a little bureaucratic hot water with inspectors over an addition he was putting on the Poplar Street building.

By the time of that 1940 census Lee Fong would have been about 70 years old. Did he die in his 60s? Did he head back to China to be with his family in his old age? Did the census taker miss him? I don't know.

'The People Have Been So Good to Me'

Whatever happened, I hope that Lee Fong's feelings for Cambridge and the Eastern Shore didn't change in the years after he returned to town, that he always felt like he did on that day in 1916 when he promised a newspaper reporter that someday he would return:

"I could not stay away," he said, "as the people are all my friends and have been so good to me. ... I just love the people and the place."

Afternote: A Chinese Feast
I asked around in search of memories of the Fongs and Star Laundry among the older set in Cambridge. I didn't get much response. Veteran downtown businessman Charles "Chip" Lednum said he recalled Star Laundry operating in his younger years, the 1950s. On Facebook a local history buff named Stan Davis offered a fun family anecdote. He remembered going to the laundry in the 1950s with his mother. They brought clothes in for cleaning, but that wasn't the real reason for the visit.

Davis's father had spent some of his younger years in China while *his* father (Davis's grandfather) was in the Navy, on assignment in Shanghai. The family had a deep familiarity with and love for authentic Chinese food. They also had an extensive collection of Chinese crockery. They had befriended the Fongs. The real reason for this visit to the laundry was that the Davises were planning to throw a big Chinese dinner party for friends. The advice they received might have come from an elderly Lee Fong, but perhaps more likely from his son, Wong/James.

Mom and I were sent to [the] laundry to discuss the menu for their dinner. [The man there] gave my mom a handwritten page of Chinese script. Mom and I then drove/ferried over to Baltimore where by appointment we met with a friendly young Chinese restaurateur named Jimmy Wu. Jimmy took the script and packed up all the ingredients for my parents' Chinese dinner party, which came off very well.

A man named Jimmy Wu had opened the New China Inn in Baltimore in 1948. He quickly became the leading Chinese restaurateur in Baltimore. The New China Inn closed in 1983, but it occupies a place of honor today in a chapter in Suzanne Loudermilk's book, *Lost Restaurants of Baltimore*.

5 INTERLUDE
THE JOURNEY OF A DEDICATED HUSBAND

There's not much left of Holland Island today, but that little spit of land in the Chesapeake Bay used to be a bigger deal, both geographically and socially. At the turn of the 20th century 360 souls lived out there between Smith and Bloodsworth Islands.

These folks had a rough go of it during a deep-freeze winter in 1905. No telephones, no telegraph lines, no radios. When the Bay froze up to the point where boats couldn't get through, Holland Islanders were cut off from the world.

They did just fine. This isn't a story about a disaster or rescue. It's a story about the dedication of a loving husband.

The Methodist minister on the island in those days was Rev. J.W. Briscoe. That deep freeze descended at a terrible time for him. His wife was sick, and she was back on the mainland, laid up in Norfolk, Va.

The old newspapers don't describe her illness, but it must have been serious, considering what Rev. Briscoe decided to do. After a few days of frozen incommunicado on the island, he couldn't take it anymore. He had to find out how his wife was doing. He had to get to her bedside. Single-digit temperatures be damned.

He bundled up as best he could and set out on a journey that would soon put his name in dozens of newspapers around the country.

• He walked six miles across the ice of a frozen Chesapeake Bay while a snowstorm was raging. He reached land in South Dorchester County.

• The boats there must have been iced in as well, because he walked another 10 miles through that weather to get to a navigable stretch of the Choptank River.

• There, he rented or borrowed a rowboat and commenced pulling his way along a river that was probably dotted with ice floes.

• Finally, he reached a real town—Cambridge. There, he hopped on a train.

• The train took him to Cape Charles, Va. He boarded a ferry for the Bay crossing to Norfolk.

His wife was doing fine. I'm sure Rev. Briscoe was happy to see her and get that news, even if it meant he'd put himself through an ordeal that maybe wasn't necessary. Somehow, a newspaper reporter got wind of what Rev. Briscoe had done. The story that reporter wrote got picked up not just by a slew of regional papers, but by publications in in Florida, Alabama, and lots of other far-flung places, including Canada.

Here's a little kicker. Do you know what day all those

stories were published? Feb. 14, 1905. I'm guessing Rev. Briscoe didn't need to get his wife a Valentine's gift for the rest of their days together, considering how he'd already gifted her with the ultimate show of dedication.

6 GOOD SAMARITAN
A PERFECT STRANGER ALONG THE UNDERGROUND RAILROAD

Don't do it. It's crazy dangerous. You'll get caught. You'll never come back.

That's the advice friends gave Harriet Tubman as she planned a 13th trip down into the slave-state danger zone. These folks knew that Harriet was an Underground Railroad conductor like no other. She'd completed a dozen missions by this point, bringing sixtysome people out of bondage.

But times had changed. By 1860 the slavery powers on the Delmarva Peninsula had had enough. Too many of "their" slaves had run off. They were on the warpath, upping rewards to bounty hunters, demanding more lawmen on the roads, and urging everyone to detain or report suspicious travelers.

Tubman knew this. But she had a bit of unfinished business. She'd already rescued four siblings, her parents, and some other relatives. One more enslaved sibling remained within her reach—a sister, Rachel.

To hell with the danger: Tubman was determined to go get her. On getting this news, fellow conductor Thomas Garrett wrote:

There is now much more risk on the road ... Wretches are constantly on the lookout [along] two roads that [Harriet] cannot well avoid. ... Yet, as it is Harriet, who seems to have had a special angel to guard her on her journey of mercy, I have hope.

In retrospect that bit about a "special angel" sounds prophetic. The story of Tubman's last ride on the Underground Railroad has Biblical qualities. Everything that could go wrong went wrong, a run of misfortune out of the Book of Job. Hey God, got any more trouble up Your sleeve?

Tubman reacted like, well, Job. She doubled down on prayer. And just when things looked hopeless, a mysterious stranger appeared. Do angels dress sometimes in dark suits and wide-brimmed hats? And do they act a little crazy to boot?

A Storm of Grief
Tubman's last ride began in heartbreak. She made her way down to Rachel's landscape on the Eastern Shore of Maryland. Tubman had grown up here in slavery. She knew the turf, and she reached out for her sister through the African American grapevine.

Word came back: Rachel was dead.

Imagine the shock. Rachel was in her mid-30s, for God's sake. The cause of death remains a mystery to historians today. Then, the grief. In an interview many years later, Harriet recalled spending one night during her "final trip" outside in the woods, all alone, huddled up against the trunk of a tree, seeking shelter from the snow and wind of a raging winter storm.

Next morning, she just got up and put that grief to the side. She shook the chill out of her bones and went back to work. She probably tried to find Rachel's two children. No such luck.

She worked that grapevine again, casting about for strangers ready to make a run at freedom. Stephen and Maria Ennals had three children in tow. The youngest was just three months old. Another guy signed on—we only know him by a first name, John.

They set off, bound for points north. But this trip was like the blues song, "Born Under a Bad Sign." The snow morphed into freezing rain. Tubman had to break out some kind of sedative to keep the two younger Ennals children quiet.

Finally, hope. Up ahead was a house that Tubman knew as an Underground Railroad station. She rapped at the door, a coded knock. Then, more bad luck. A white man appeared at the window, telling Tubman that the black man she had expected to find had been "obliged to leave" over suspicions that he was helping runaways.

Day was breaking. Even in a storm, Tubman knew, suspicious, watchful eyes would be out on nearby roads. What if that white man at the window reported her visit to authorities? Without that black station master, Tubman likely wasn't sure where to go in search of the next helping hand.

'These Sudden Deliverances'

People who write about Tubman's incredible accomplishments (myself included, in a book titled *Tubman Travels: 32 Underground Railroad Journeys on Delmarva*) often go a tad over the top, turning Tubman into a superhero out of the movies, responding to each new bit of danger with this brilliant plan or that clever trick.

Not this time. She had nothing up her sleeve.

She retreated. She found a nearby stretch of marsh with a patch of high land surrounded by water. The freezing and exhausted fugitives waded out and climbed onto the island. There,

54

they could at least keep out of sight behind "tall and rank" grasses.

But how long would they last? They needed food. Blankets, too. Wouldn't a horse-drawn wagon be nice? Tubman's experiences on 12 previous trips had given her a well-honed instinct for danger. Everything about this moment told her: Stay put. Don't budge.

An hour passed, then two, then ten. Still, the freezing rain came down. Tubman's plan amounted to this: Pray. From Tubman biographer Sarah Bradford, whose books were based on interviews with Harriet:

Her faith never wavered, her silent prayer still ascended, and she confidently expected help from some quarter or other.

Then, at dusk, a man appeared on the mainland. He must have had a ghostly aspect—Tubman said it was hard to make out his features in the low light. He was acting quite strangely. He walked along the path at the water's edge for a bit, then turned around and retraced his steps. He did it again. And again. And again.

Wait, was he muttering to himself?

Perhaps Tubman had to inch toward the edge of the island, risking exposing her hideout. From here, even in that fading light, she finally made out what he looked like. With that dark suit and low-brimmed hat, could he be a Quaker? Such "Friends" were often helpful to runaways.

Then, perhaps when the wind blew just right, Harriet made out the words he was muttering over and over again:

My wagon stands in the barnyard of the farm across the way. The

55

horse is in the stable. The harness hangs on a nail.

Could he be trusted? Was he the answer to her prayers? Tubman took a chance. After nightfall she told her fugitives to lay low while she waded across the water. There was a barn. The wagon inside really was ready to roll. Better yet, it was stocked with food, blankets, and other necessities.

She and the Ennals family and John rode that wagon hard through the night, finding their way somehow or another to friends along the Underground Railroad. Along the way Harriet picked up another couple of fugitives. All eight made it to freedom in the north.

Harriet Tubman never learned the name of this Good Samaritan. She never got to say thank you. Historians can't put a name on this hero.

Figuring out what happened isn't rocket science. The man must have seen that gaggle of desperate fugitives and understood their predicament. He must have decided to step up and risk his own freedom to help them. As a Quaker, he likely did this in the spirit of his faith. Quakers had been the first religious group to condemn slavery. The ranks of Underground Railroad heroes are chock full of "Friends."

Still, it's hard to dismiss the notion that something else was at work. A ghostly figure appears at dusk, acting like a crazy man, just when hope is all but lost. Really? Here again is Tubman biographer Sarah Bradford:

These sudden deliverances never seemed to strike her as at all strange or mysterious. Her prayer was the prayer of faith and she expected an answer.

7 KINDNESS
THE UNLIKELY HERO: HOW HENRY CALLISTER SAVED THE REFUGEES

The 200 or so souls aboard the *Ranger* were in desperate straits when the sloop sailed out of Annapolis on Dec. 8, 1755. Hungry, exhausted, penniless. Many dreadfully sick, some on the verge of death. None spoke English. The *Ranger* headed down the Chesapeake Bay, then up the Choptank River and into the Tred Avon. She landed in the town of Oxford, Md.

The captain dumped those poor souls on the dock and sailed away. None of the locals had any warning this crisis was coming. It's easy to imagine their reaction:

You can't just drop a boatload of strange, deathly sick people here! The government needs to fix this! It isn't our job!

I don't mean that description as criticism. Think about it: What would your reaction be if you woke one morning and found someone had dumped a load of hungry, broke foreigners on your block? There might be calls to the police and the mayor involved, no? Maybe some F-bombs flying around?

Next question: Who in your neighborhood would be the first to step past that initial outrage and pay attention to the human crisis? You're probably thinking of a do-gooder on the block, the neighbor who tends to the needs of stray animals, say, or the one who picks up litter and volunteers at the church soup kitchen.

It's a safe guess that no one in Oxford back in 1755 would have picked Henry Callister as a man likely to step into a saintly role. The immigrant from Great Britain had a huge ego. He could be quite a snob. The local rumor mill pegged him as a womanizer. He'd done some petty, underhanded things in his business dealings. His bosses worried that he had a drinking problem.

And yet ... there is Callister's name, written prominently in a testimonial signed by a good number of those desperate refugees many months after the *Ranger* stranded them in Oxford.

We were reduced to die of hunger, saving the assistance of Mr. Callister. We can say with truth that he has saved our lives.

Let's try and figure this out, shall we?

History Rhymes: Of Migrants, Buses, and Sloops
Mark Twain penned the famous aphorism, "History doesn't repeat itself, but it rhymes." Case in point: Newspapers in the early 2020s were full of reports about busloads of needy migrants getting dumped off here and there—in Washington DC, New York City, Chicago, and even on Martha's Vineyard.

The story behind these busloads of controversy starts in foreign lands, with migrants fleeing tough times and seeking better lives by trekking through remote jungles in Colombia and high deserts in Mexico to enter the United States illegally. Their arrival soon becomes a political hot potato as leaders in Southern border states that have been bearing the brunt of caring for such new arrivals decide that perhaps it would be better if that burden was shared by other states and locales. So they loaded up buses, which are soon dropping migrants off without warning in far-off cities.

So it was with Oxford's shipload of controversy. The French and Indian War of the 1750s and 1760s unfolded far from the Delmarva Peninsula, up in Canada and over on the western "frontier" of Pennsylvania and Ohio. The conflict was the North American piece of a much larger Seven Years War. Nearly every European country got caught up in that. High-seas cannon fire rang out all over the Atlantic world. Battles erupted as far away as Asia.

What the *Ranger* did was drop off a piece of that war in Oxford. Below is the sequence of events that led up to that December day in 1755.

• French settlers first arrived in Nova Scotia in 1604. They set up camp around the Bay of Fundy. They set about building dikes and running irrigation ditches that would transform an economically unattractive place into such fertile farmland that it became known as Acadia—the "place of abundance."

• The French king basically forgot about these settlers, leaving them to fend for themselves. The English ignored them, too, after claiming control of the area in 1714.

• Living independently through several generations in a wild New World, the Fundy French morphed into a people apart, with their own unique culture and traditions.

• That notion that land in places like Nova Scotia officially "belonged" to France or England was more a mirage of European paperwork than on-the-ground reality. The real power around the Bay of Fundy lay with the Mi'kmaq Indian nation. They had the strongest military. Their foreign policy decisions shaped the political realities and trading practices of the area.

• And so the Fundy French worked hard to nurture friendship and goodwill with the Mi'kmaqs.

• By the early 1700s France and Great Britain were bickering over this, that, and some other things. Those fights soon spilled over into their North American territories. The Brits who now claimed to "own" Nova Scotia started eyeing the Fundy French with suspicion. What would they do if war broke out with France? Or with the Mi'kmaq? Or with both? Would they betray us?

• To calm things down the Fundy French agreed to play like modern-day Switzerland and swear an oath of neutrality in the event of hostilities.

• The drums of war grew louder. The French built a new fort in a place the Brits regarded as too close for comfort. The Brits responded with a new fort of their own. The French built yet another fort. And so on.

• When hostilities erupted most of the Fundy French lived up to their promise of neutrality.

• But there were exceptions. When the Brits attacked and conquered one of those French forts, they found inside a few Fundy Frenchmen who had been collaborating with the "enemy."

That changed everything. British governor Charles Lawrence did not mess around upon hearing this news. He demanded that every Fundy Frenchman go beyond those old neutrality oaths and pledge full allegiance to Great Britain. The Fundy Frenchmen refused. By most accounts they did that less out of loyalty to a far-away French king and more out of fear of losing their friendship with their Mi'kmaq neighbors. To oversimplify their thinking:

If we swear allegiance to the Brits, how would that affect our relationship with the real power around here, the Mi'kmaqs? It might well be the end of us if we are forced by this deal to fight the Indians.

What happened next may or may not qualify as a "crime against humanity" in the modern-day legal sense—different historians have different answers to that question. Gov. Lawrence decided to round up the Fundy French and ship them off to … somewhere, anywhere, who cares where, as long as it was far away. One of Gov. Lawrence's minions appeared before the Fundy French and read this proclamation:

That your Land & Tennements, Cattle of all Kinds and Livestocks of all Sorts are forfeited to the Crown with all other your effects Savings your money and Household Goods, and you yourselves to be removed from this Province.

Translation: The governor planned to steal everything the Fundy

French owned and deport them by force. Most historians suspect that greed played a part in this decision. Some British settlers down in New England had their eye on the fertile farmland the Fundy French had created with those dikes and irrigation ditches. Why, the New Englanders argued, should such prime land belong to potentially disloyal "aliens?"

British troops surrounded various Fundy French settlements, one by one. Some of those greedy New Englanders pitched in on the operation, too. One notorious capture happened while the Fundy French were in church celebrating Roman Catholic mass. The Fundy watched helplessly as soldiers burnt their houses and crops. They got herded into captivity at the point of bayonets. One historian:

They went reluctantly, praying, singing, and crying.

Historians know this tragic chapter by a variety of names: the "Great Upheaval," "the Great Deportation," or "the Expulsion of the Acadians." Spoiler alert: After enduring this exodus from their homeland, many Fundy French survivors slowly but surely made their way to the swamps and cities of Louisiana. They are the ancestors of our modern-day Cajuns.

Between 1755 and 1763 more than 10,000 Fundy French got shipped off to various British ports, many in the American colonies, but others in more distant locales, like islands in the Caribbean. By some estimates as many as half of these men, women, and children died during and in the aftermath of these voyages—of infectious disease, of starvation, and in shipwrecks.

Several boatloads of this controversy landed in Maryland's capital, Annapolis. Colonial officials there felt that this was too much for them to handle. So, in the manner of our modern-day Southern border states and their busloads of immigrants, the powers that be in Annapolis decided that other Maryland towns should share in the burden.

This passing of the buck is how the *Ranger* came to Oxford, dropping off that desperate human cargo and then skedaddling without so much as a fare-thee-well.

More Rhyming: The Terrorism Scare of 1755

Do you recall the days after the 9/11 attacks on New York and Washington in 2001? How our newspapers and TV screens were filled with vague, terrifying reports about this or that terrorist "cell" and this or that rumored "second-wave" attack on the horizon?

The French and Indian War created that kind of atmosphere in Maryland, especially after British troops under Major General Edward Braddock suffered an ignominious defeat to a mixed force of French and Indian soldiers in the Battle of Monongahela in western Pennsylvania. That happened in July 1755, just a few months before the *Ranger* arrived in Oxford.

Maryland had only one real newspaper at the time, the *Gazette*. In the months that followed that battle its pages were filled with reports—almost all false, but readers didn't know that—about nefarious plotting by French and Indian enemies and the brutal atrocities they loved to commit. Historian Basil Sollers:

Terror seems for a time to have taken possession of the people and all sorts of rumors were circulated and believed.

One example among many to choose from in the pages of the *Gazette*:

Ordinary Heroes of Old Delmarva

The Indian Enemy now are within a little way of us, and while the main body keep together, 'tis very possible, nay highly probable, that a small Party of Twenty or Thirty of these, marching in the Night, and skulking in the Day-time, may come upon us unaware in the Dead of night, burn our Houses, and Cut our Throats, before we can put ourselves in any posture of Defence.

Another report placed a band of enemies within 30 miles of Baltimore. Citizens in that city hastily put together a paramilitary defense unit. Angry Philadelphians nearly tore down a Roman Catholic "Mass house" frequented by French residents and visitors. On the outskirts of Annapolis citizens banded together and started digging defensive trenches for use during the attacks they expected any day now.

So the air was thick with fear by the time news broke that the Fundy French were getting deported from Nova Scotia. On the appropriately rhyming date of Sept. 11, 1755, the *Gazette* published a letter from a guy up in Canada describing the operation British officials had embarked on:

We are now upon a great and noble Scheme of sending the Neutral French out of this Province, who have always been secret Enemies, and have encouraged our Savages to cut our Throats. If we effect their Expulsion, it will be one of the greatest Things that ever the English did in America, for by all the accounts that Part of the Country they possess is as good Land as any in the World. In case therefore we could get some good English Farmers in their Room, this Province would abound with all kinds of Provisions.

By early December the Canadian Brits had shipped nearly 1,000

Fundy French refugees to Annapolis. In a letter prominent lawyer and politician Daniel Dulany summed up the feelings of most folks in the city:

What is to be done with these people? God knows.

No one with authority was offering to pay for food, shelter, and medical care—not the king in England, not the British army in Nova Scotia. The colonial authorities in Annapolis passed the buck as well. They distributed refugees to nearly every county in the state, including several Eastern Shore counties. When the Fundy French landed in Oxford, this was the sum total of guidance that arrived with them:

[Do with these people] as Charity inclines [you] to receive them. It remains with you to dispose of them otherwise or provide for their support as you shall judge proper.

Henry Callister and the 'Seeds of Our Humanity'

Different sources give different numbers of Fundy French on the *Ranger*—it's safe to say there were somewhere between 181 and 263 refugees aboard. The historical sources all agree on this: Locals reacted to the refugees' arrival with a mix of outrage, fear, and throw-up-your-hands helplessness.

Many Oxford residents disparaged the refugees for their strange Roman Catholic faith and judged them guilty by linguistic association with the French enemy. Others fretted that the foreigners would try to foment rebellion among slaves and/or local Indians.

Still others jumped into the weeds of a complicated legal debate: Were the refugees prisoners of war as legally defined in various treaties? If so, the British army should be required by law to care for them! Some folks fired off letters trying to make that case to Annapolis. At least one wrote directly to the king of England. Nothing came of all that back and forth.

Meanwhile, the refugees were hungry and homeless. Many were deathly ill. Winter was coming on fast.

Born in England in 1717 Henry Callister received a reasonably good education as a child, then learned the ropes of the 18th century trading world while apprenticing as a young adult with businesses in Ireland and France. What brought him across the Atlantic was a job opportunity: He accepted a gig as a "factor," facilitating trade deals and shipping arrangements for a British mercantile firm called Foster Cunliffe.

His first assignment was in Cambridge, Md. That went south when he fell in love with a young woman who spurned his advances over rumors—who knows if they were true?—about his supposed multiple illicit affairs and womanizing ways. That blowup led Foster Cunliffe to pull him out of Cambridge and transfer him to Oxford. He didn't qualify as a big man in town, but he did get to hang out with the social upper crust.

He was a bit of a snob about this, especially when it came to arts and culture in his new home as compared with that of his native England. Here is one bit from a letter he wrote about the musical talent on display at the town's then-popular weekly jam sessions.

You must know that we abound in fiddlers, but most wretched ones they are. Some of the better sort have a little of the true taste, but they are content if they exceed the vulgar in that, and seldom get any further.

Five years before the *Ranger* arrived, Oxford had endured a terrible civic loss when its leading citizen, Robert Morris Sr., died in a bizarre accident involving the firing of a cannon for ceremonial purposes. Morris had been in charge of local operations at Foster Cunliffe.

Callister's place in the company didn't put him anywhere near next-in-line status, but he immediately began plotting against the odds to snag Morris's old position. Historian Dickson Preston:

In so doing [Callister] revealed traits in his character of pettiness and greed. ... [He seemed to have] more egotism than judgment.

The Foster Cunliffe bosses back in England didn't fall for Callister's scheming. Five years later, when the *Ranger* dropped off those Fundy French refugees, he was still just another one among several company "factors." Callister agreed with his neighbors about some aspects of that shipload of controversy. He thought authorities somewhere—whether Annapolis, Nova Scotia, or England—should foot the bill for their care. He agreed that as a rule French-speaking Catholics were not to be trusted, since "Papist principles are dangerous."

But he also felt this:

Our aversion to their principles must not be allowed to destroy the seeds of [our] humanity.

The Fundy French Find Their Savior
The first thing Callister did to live up to this notion of shared "humanity" was reach into his pocket to buy food and other essentials for the refugees. He kept records of all those expenses, figuring (wrongly, as it turned out) that some government body

somewhere down the line would come to its senses, take responsibility, and reimburse him.

Next he set out to convince his neighbors to pitch in. He found a helping hand in Rev. Thomas Bacon, the pastor at nearby Whitemarsh Church. On Sunday, Dec. 14 Bacon preached a sermon that included a heartfelt plea for generosity in a special collection for the refugees. It didn't go over well:

Reflecting the sentiment of many of the townsfolk, the contribution of Reverend Bacon [himself] exceeded that of the rest of his congregation.

Callister kept plugging away. He took refugees into his own home. He got Rev. Bacon to take some in as well. Perhaps other townsfolk agreed to this—there isn't a detailed record of which refugees stayed where. But after all that arm-twisting around town there were still more refugees in Oxford than there were places for them to sleep and meals for them to eat.

Callister got creative. One way to think about this: Perhaps that deviousness he had developed in past romantic and business dealings paid off in this moment of crisis. He used his Foster Cunliffe business connections to commission a young sailor named Jeremiah Banning to load refugees aboard the schooner *Humming Bird* and sail up the Wye River, which just so happened to be where some of the Eastern Shore's biggest and most luxurious estates were set.

Banning sailed from rich-guy dock to rich-guy dock, dropping a few refugees off at every stop. It's possible that some of those rich guys knew this was coming and had agreed to it, but some of them had cut no such deal. Dickson Preston again:

Apparently without asking permission, Banning landed a number of them at Wye House, the Lloyd home, further infuriating the irascible Edward Lloyd, who fired off a letter to London asking that Lord Baltimore be informed of this outrage.

The Lloyds ranked as the closest thing to royalty in Maryland in those years. Edward Lloyd was no fan of the Fundy French. He didn't think they should be his problem. He fretted about the evil "Papists" who would probably soon be about the business of "corrupting mine & other Negroe slaves" with talk of revolution. But in a surprise twist Callister's scam worked. Lloyd ended up housing several refugees, though he presumably made the healthy ones earn their keep by working his lands. In the end Lloyd even agreed to contribute a few pounds a week toward a fund Callister had established to help sick and helpless refugees.

Other rich guys did their part too. Capt. Banning and the crew on the *Humming Bird* dropped human cargo off at estates associated with some of the most famous names in Talbot County history—the Tilghmans at Rich Neck, the Hambletons at Martingham, and the Chamberlaines at Plain Dealing. By the time Callister and Banning wrapped this operation up, there were only 30 refugees left in Oxford, and they were all "taken care of in one way or another."

It wasn't a perfect solution, but at least it got all the refugees fed and housed in the short term. Even with roofs over their heads the refugees had to endure injustices. Some were kept as virtual prisoners by their suspicious keepers. They were required to carry travel passes in order to go anywhere unescorted.

Almost two years later, in 1757, the refugees were still a source of frustration in the Talbot County community. A group of citizens petitioned the legislature in Annapolis, begging them to do something "to have this pest removed from amongst us." At least a few of the Fundy French were still unemployed and hungry at this point.

[They were] going from house to house begging, whereby they are become a nuisance.

County authorities eventually imposed a tax designed to raise enough money to provide some bare-bones relief, but only families with children or old people in clear danger of starvation qualified to receive anything. The colonial authorities in Annapolis never did agree to do anything for the refugees. Neither did the British Army, or the king of England.

The Refugees Join the American Journey
In time the crisis passed. Some Fundy French stayed on the Eastern Shore, melting into the local populations by getting jobs and acquiring land and even becoming prominent citizens. Some of their descendants would fight in the American Revolution—this time with the French as our allies.

But most of the refugees left after hearing through the grapevine about the way some of their former neighbors in Nova Scotia who'd been strewn hither and yon were re-gathering down in Louisiana, where lots of folks spoke French and some old Fundy folks were trying to create a new Acadian "place of abundance."

Without a doubt, then, some Cajuns in Louisiana today are descended from Oxford refugees. Their ancestors might well have left the Eastern Shore owing their lives to the crisis-response magic worked by an unlikely hero. Was Henry Callister a greedy, heavy-drinking, snob of a womanizer who ran some shady business deals? Maybe. But he was also a man who found his way to doing the right thing by his notion of our shared "humanity" at a time when his Oxford neighbors weren't up to the task.

Hey, maybe there's hope yet for a heroic turn in life by all of us sinners!

Afternote: What the Acadians Saw
Here's a bit of trivia for those of you who've been to Oxford and seen the sights. Those poor Fundy French refugees saw some things in the 1750s that can still be seen in and around Oxford today.

The Oxford-Bellevue Ferry that runs today across the Tred Avon River dates its history to the 1680s. Parts of the Robert Morris Inn, a modern-day landmark, date to 1710. Partial ruins of the old Whitemarsh Episcopal Church where Rev. Thomas Bacon begged parishioners to help the refugees are still standing along modern-day Route 50 a little way south of Easton. The original building there dates to the 1650s.

8 COMMUNITY
'BE KIND TO ALL LIVING CREATURES'

Pass by a restaurant or shop in one of the small towns on the Delmarva peninsula and you might see a big bowl of water tucked out of the way in a corner of the sidewalk for dogs in need of water. I don't remember such bowls being around much—if at all—in my childhood years. I used to think of it as a little sign that maybe the world is a kinder place than it used to be.

That was before I learned that a gaggle of schoolgirls in Ridgely, Md. put that little gesture to shame back in 1914.

Folks in Ridgely were still getting around in carriages and on horseback at that time. Automobiles were few and far between. Henry Ford was just getting started with the mass production lines that would make Model Ts affordable to regular folks. Farmers brought crops into town aboard heavy wagons pulled by oxen or mules.

Some of those beasts of burden weighed more than 1,000 pounds. A little bowl wasn't going to quench their thirst. They needed a giant trough. Shop owners couldn't help with that. Troughs would block the sidewalk. They'd be a pain to refill. They'd slop up the shoes of customers. They'd be a breeding ground for mosquitoes. Here is from a historic marker that stands today in Ridgely:

Strangers passing through town [were] compelled to get water [for their animals] from backyards and other private places.

Who would step up? How about a band of little schoolgirls? They dubbed themselves the "Forget-me-not Band of Mercy." They launched a fundraising campaign in April 1914 to build and install a humongous water fountain that emptied into a trough in the middle of town. It would be plenty big enough to slake the thirst of those beasts of burden.

'Say a Kind Word,' 'Do a Kind Act'

The girls were part of a nationwide movement that historians regard as the birth of our modern animal-welfare advocates. A fledgling organization called the Society for the Prevention of Cruelty to Animals took its first baby steps in Boston in the late 1800s. In that same window a group of women led by Caroline Earle White founded the first modern-style animal shelter in Bensalem, Pa.

Then there were the "Bands of Mercy." That name wasn't unique to Ridgely. The term has roots in the anti-alcohol temperance movement. Members of "Bands of Hope" chapters pledged to never drink alcohol. Early animal welfare reformers copied that structure, forming bands of mercy in towns around the country—and beyond. The first Band of Mercy popped up in Great Britain, actually.

By the early 1900s there were 27,000 Band of Mercy chapters operating across North America, with a combined membership of more than 260,000—most of them children between the ages of five and nine. Here is the mission statement of those clubs:

To teach and lead every child and older person to seize every opportunity to say a kind word or do a kind act that will make some other human being or some dumb creature happier.

That word *dumb* was not meant as an insult. It was used in the sense not of being stupid, but of being unable to talk. Every member made this pledge:

I will try to be kind to all living creatures and try to protect them from cruel usage.

There was a national newspaper called the *Band of Mercy Advocate* that reported on the activities of various clubs. Two books of hymns and songs were published especially for the clubs, with tunes written "to bring language—and aesthetically pleasing language at that—to a population of animals unable to speak in their own defense."

The Band of Mercy movement peaked in the early 1900s, then went into a slow, steady decline as the nation and the world endured World War I, the Great Depression, and World War II. The movement was pretty much dead by the 1950s.

'In the Name of Love and Mercy'

Ridgely's Forget-me-not Band of Mercy got to work quickly. Just 10 weeks after announcing the club's formation, the girls threw a big midsummer carnival. The grounds were "brilliantly lit" with electric lights. There were "booths of all kinds," a "famous gypsy" telling fortunes, a fish pond "where real fish live," and a "country store." The headline gimmick was rides in one of those newfangled automobiles at five cents a pop.

In November they threw a Halloween party, raising $72 ("of which fifty-seven dollars and twenty-two cents was clear"). There were "recitations" and "shadow pictures" a "witch drill," and a "pumpkin drill" on a stage decorated with corn stalks. Refreshments included ginger cake, grapes, coffee, and cocoa. The *Denton Journal* newspaper on Nov. 7, 1914 included some details on the affair that might make modern-day readers cringe in ways that folks back then weren't focused on.

The Hallowe'en fete held by the Forget-me-not Band of Mercy was a decided success. The march of the maskers, about forty in number, afforded much merriment. The prize for the best costume was awarded to Miss Virginia Holt, costumed as an Indian squaw, and accompanied by an Indian brave. The prize for the funniest costume went to a huge colored "mammy."

The girls put on a carnival at some point, then put together a big party the following February. The *Denton Journal*, Feb. 6, 1915:

The Band of Mercy gives an entertainment at Simon's Hall next Tuesday evening. Our people have learned to expect something good when the Band of Mercy entertains.

After one short year of throwing parties the girls had raised all the money they needed. When the big day arrived on May 15, 1915, the town turned out in force to cheer the girls on. The *Denton Journal*:

The public drinking fountain for which our Band of Mercy has been working so long has been installed, the event being ... witnessed by a large number of people last Saturday evening.

The town band provided musical entertainment. Rev. Harvey Holsinger said a blessing. Everyone joined in singing, "Maryland My Maryland." Rev. A.M. Rahn sang the praises of the girls' work. W.E. Abbart read aloud from a scroll that gave a history of the Forget-me-not Band of Mercy and listed the names of all the girls in the club. That scroll was then sealed into the base of the fountain in time-capsule fashion.

The guest of honor was a "very old horse" named "General." His owner, Thomas Temple, rode him up to the fountain. General drank up, "amid much applause."

The fountain had this inscription on it:

In the name of Love and Mercy to all God's creatures.

Afternote
The Band of Mercy's fountain still stands in Ridgely today, refurbished and repainted. Find it where Central Avenue meets the railroad tracks in the heart of town. It's on the west side, along Railroad Avenue. A historic marker about the project is on other side of the tracks, along West Belle Street.

9 INGENUITY
A DELAWARE MAN SHOVELS HIS WAY TO RICHES

"Gold, boys, gold!"

When that cry of joy rang out in Coloma, Calif. on Jan. 24, 1848, the response was ... well ... not much, at least not right away. Times were different. Consider:

• California still belonged to Mexico. The Mexican-American War was winding down, and the Treaty of Guadalupe that would move California into the American column didn't get signed until February. The guys negotiating that treaty were down near Mexico City, oblivious to the news.

• No internet, no railroad, no telegraph: News traveled slowly. Folks in San Francisco heard the rumors first, but they were skeptical, having been through false gold alarms before. They finally came around that spring when a guy named Samuel Brannan showed up, running through the streets and screaming "Gold! Gold! Gold from the American River!" He was waving a jar of the stuff over his head.

• By summertime a huge chunk of San Francisco's male population had run off in search of gold.

• Guys from Hawaii, Oregon, Mexico, and even China showed up next. All those places got the news long before it arrived on the East Coast.

• No one along the Atlantic Coast believed early rumors, either, as they mostly came from random lay people who'd maybe heard about the find in a letter from a cousin or some such.

• Finally, on Dec. 5, 1848, President James Polk informed Congress that the rumors were true.

From Sussex County to Stockton

All heck broke loose. Thousands of East Coast men borrowed money, mortgaged homes, and ran through their life savings to finance the trip to California. Most left wives and kids behind. Those women and children soon found themselves in new roles, running farms and managing small businesses.

Eye-popping numbers: California had 7,000 non-Native-American (mostly European) residents on the day gold was discovered. By the end of the following year, 1849, it had 100,000 non-native residents.

Among the new arrivals was an enterprising young man from Sussex County, Delaware. Born in Lewes in 1818, Harbeson Hickman was around 30 years old when the gold rush began. He'd done okay for himself to that point in life, having partnered with a brother in a wholesale hardware operation in Philadelphia.

He sold his stake in that operation upon hearing the siren

song of California gold. The journey he and thousands of other men took from the East Coast to California will sound insane to modern ears, but, as I already noted, times were different.

The travelers had two choices. One, hop on a boat and sail around the tip of South America, covering nearly 20,000 miles in an era long before the arrival of seasickness medications. Two, take the hybrid route. Sail down the Atlantic to Panama, which did not yet have a canal. Get off and tromp through a disease-infested jungle to the shores of the Pacific. If you made it in good health, you'd board another ship for the run up to San Francisco.

Hickman chose the longer route, aboard a vessel named *Algoma*. One possible reason is that he might have been traveling with a whole bunch of luggage, far too much to drag through that Panamanian jungle.

Hickman had no intention of panning or digging for gold. He either brought along a big supply of hardware goods—buckets, shovels, pick-axes, you name it—or he carried enough cash to buy a slew of tools upon arriving in California.

He settled in the town of Stockton and opened a hardware store.

'Thousands Will Leave Their Bones Here'

As exciting as a "gold rush" sounds in theory, the guys chasing that dream in the 1850s faced a harsh life with poor prospects. No high-tech mining inventions had appeared yet. The "placer mining" techniques they employed were centuries old at this point. That meant hunting for gold that had broken away from its natural geological home in rock formations. Such nuggets, flakes, grains, and gold dust turned up mostly in stream beds or in places that used to be stream beds, like canyons.

Picks and shovels were key tools in their long days of

manual labor, along with specialty items with names like "cradles" and "long toms."

The odds of winning the gold rush game were low from the get-go, but they got lower and lower as time went on. That long delay in the news making it across the country meant that most of the easy-to-find stuff was gone by the time East Coast guys arrived.

Mostly, miners lived in tents. If they snagged a spot in a tiny cabin, they were likely rooming with five or six other guys. Here is how one of those miners summed up the bleak reality of gold rush life:

Many, very many, that come here meet with bad success and thousands will leave their bones here. Others will lose their health, contract diseases that they will carry to their graves ... Some will have to beg their way home and probably one half ... will never make enough [money] to carry them back [home].

Who knows how many of Harbeson Hickman's neighbors on the Delmarva Peninsula ended up in those desperate straits? Scores? Hundreds? More?

By contrast, Harbeson Hickman's hardware-store plan worked to perfection. His story personifies a business-world maxim that still pops up nowadays, nearly two centuries later, in advice books for entrepreneurs.

During a gold rush, sell shovels.

Hickman made a fortune during his 10-year California sojourn. As the gold rush slowed down after four or five years, he started speculating in California real estate. By the time he moved back home to Delaware he was, well, richer than God.

'The Richest Man in Sussex County'

He was married, too. He met Eliza aboard a ship in the midst of his gold rush sojourn, while returning to Stockton after a visit home to Delaware in the wake of his father's death. Eliza's mother had died recently. She was traveling west to move in with a relative. The fact that she was 13 years old didn't stop the thirty-something Hickman from falling head over heels. Did I mention that times were different?

He waited until Eliza was 16 or 17 before tying the knot. They would eventually have four children together.

Back in Delaware Hickman stuck with the real estate game. Once again his timing was perfect. Quite a few Southern Delaware farmers landed in financial trouble in the 1860s—they had mismanaged their land and worn out their soils. Hickman picked up bargains in foreclosure, eventually owning more than 5,000 acres and renting the land out to tenant farmers.

He got into shipping, too, investing in at least 10 and perhaps as many as 40 vessels that sailed trading routes to the West Indies, South America, Europe, and beyond. One of those ships bore his name—the three-masted schooner *Harbeson Hickman* was built in Milford in 1874. (Keep reading to the end here for a strange little tidbit about that vessel that will be of interest to UFO aficionados.)

Hickman put his fortune to use in various civic and political causes. He donated land to a pair of church groups in a fledgling town near his native Lewes that eventually took his first name, Harbeson. The blink-and-you'll-miss-it town of Hickman (northwest of Greenwood, along Route 16) might be named after him as well, though some folks suspect that name honors another family member.

He helped promote farming innovation through a group called the Seaside Agricultural Association. He served as a bank director and in various Democratic Party leadership roles. He tried to build a big fairground near Harbeson, but that never really took off.

When Hickman died in 1890 the *Wilmington Morning News* dubbed him "the richest man in Sussex County." He had reached that height by thinking creatively, seeing more clearly than most everyone else where the real get-rich-quick opportunities lay in the frenzied days of the California Gold Rush.

Afternote: The UFO Connection

In 1891 the *Harbeson Hickman* set sail for Martinique with a load of coal. She ran into a terrible storm, then disappeared. Newspapers in the Delmarva region and beyond reported the ship lost and presumed sunk.

But the *Harbeson Hickman* made a surprising reappearance, docking in Martinique. Woo-boy did that crew have a story to tell! These excerpts are from an account in the *Philadelphia Inquirer* that has drawn attention lately in our modern-day community of UFO obsessives.

• *She ran into a terrific gale from the south, accompanied by heavy seas that lasted twelve hours.*

• *[But then an] extraordinary sunset riveted the attention of all hands.*

• *Immediately after a huge mass of black clouds appeared as if by magic, and in its center was a small ball of fire which appeared to revolve as it constantly changed its formation.*

• *This phenomenon lasted two hours, during which a strange roaring sound was heard above the swish of the water around the ship's sides.*

The *Harbeson Hickman* was eventually transformed into a barge, working waters up near Connecticut in the early 1900s. After springing a leak in 1911, she was dismantled. The only piece of her that survives is a name board—it's in the collection of the Mystic Seaport Museum in Mystic, Connecticut.

10 INDEFATIGABLE
MEET THE MOTHER OF THE CENTURY

Let's take a break from this Delmarva landscape and pay a brief visit to Toronto. Up there you'll find a street called Albert Jackson Lane. A historical marker tells tourists why Albert Jackson is worth remembering. The Canadian postal service issued a stamp in Jackson's honor. A mega-warehouse where international mail gets sorted is called the Albert Jackson Processing Centre.

An old saying is relevant here: Behind every great man is a great woman. In this case, Ann Maria Jackson.

A Family Ripped Apart
Ann Maria gave birth to Albert Jackson sometime around 1856 back on our Delmarva Peninsula, in Milford, Del. Albert was either the youngest or close to it of the nine children this enslaved woman had with her husband, John.

John, a blacksmith, was legally "free." But that meant nothing when it came to the status of Ann Maria and her children, as ownership status passed through mothers, not fathers. Ann Maria and her children were the legal property of a wealthy widower named Joseph Brown, who lived mostly in Milford but also had property in Mississippi. Brown was tall, slim, and bald. He had light hair and a long, sharp nose. Ann once described him as man with a fondness for drinking and a penchant for cursing.

Brown seems to have had a good thing going for himself with the Jacksons. He allowed Ann and her children to live away from his property, with her husband and their father, on condition that they do their work and otherwise support themselves. Ann pitched in on this front by hiring herself out as a laundress and taking on other odd jobs in addition to her slave-labor duties.

But Brown wanted more. When Ann Maria's two oldest boys hit an age where they were able to put in a day's work, he moved them away from their home, assigning them to a different Delaware slave owner for an annual fee. Ann Maria:

It almost broke my heart. He came and took my children away as soon as they were big enough to hand me a drink of water.

She tried at this point to convince her husband that they should make a run for the North, where the family might live together in freedom. John didn't go for that plan, but neither did he get over the heartbreak of losing two children. He suffered some sort of mental breakdown, the loss of those kids preying

so severely on the poor father's mind that it drove him into a state of hopeless insanity. He died in the poor house, a raving maniac.

Freedom, Against All Odds
That was in 1858. The brutal one-two punch of losing two children and a husband left a grieving Ann Maria thinking again about making a break for freedom. But was an escape even possible? She still had seven children at home, the youngest a toddler.

The breaking point came later in that same year of 1858 when Ann Maria heard through the grapevine that her owner planned to relocate four more of her children, this time even farther away, to Mississippi.

I just happened to hear of this news. My master was wanting to keep me in the dark about taking them.

Now she decided she had to flee. But what kind of chance did she have? Fleeing slavery with seven children in tow? Historians John Hope Franklin and Loren Schweninger laid out some of the challenges on that horizon:

It was not easy to feed, clothe, care for, and protect children while on the run. The physical burden of carrying babies or youngsters four or five years of age was extreme, while seven- or eight-year-olds had trouble keeping up and often tired quickly.

It's not clear whether Ann Maria made connections in advance with activists in the Underground Railroad, or if she happened upon that network while in flight. At one point in the family's journey through Delaware, Ann Maria was sure that she had been betrayed, but, as one Underground Railroad activist put it later,

She was lucky enough to fall into the right hands.

Soon the Jacksons were moving under the watchful eye of Thomas Garrett, a legendary conductor based in Wilmington, Del. Here is a report that he sent during the heat of the escape:

We had some trouble in getting [the Jacksons] safe along, as they

could not travel far on foot, and could not safely cross any of the bridges on the canal, either on foot or in carriage. A man left here two days since, with carriage, to meet them this side of the canal, but owing to spies they did not reach him till 10 o'clock last night; this morning he returned, having seen them about one or two o'clock this morning in a second carriage, on the border of Chester County, [Pennsylvania] where I think they are all safe. ... May He, who feeds the ravens, care for them.

He who feeds the ravens did just that. The Jacksons eventually made their way to the Philadelphia office of William Still. Many of the quotes here are from the journal Still kept of his time with the Philadelphia Anti-Slavery Society, where his job was to help runaways who had successfully made it across the border and into Pennsylvania get resettled somewhere farther to the north.

'The Fire of Freedom'
Still described Ann Maria Jackson as a "good looking" woman of about 40 years. She was of "medium" height. Her skin was "chestnut" colored. "Her bearing was humble," but her intellect was clearly "above average." Still asked Ann Maria about her day-to-day life.

Year in and year out she had suffered to provide food and raiment for her little ones. Many times in going out to do a day's work she would be compelled to leave her children, not knowing whether during her absence they would fall victims to fire or be carried off by the master.

Still cited Ann Maria's faith in God when discussing her remark-able strength and courage. The most memorable line in his account of the family is this:

The fire of freedom obviously burned with no ordinary fervor in the breast of this slave mother.

On Nov. 20, 1858 William Still received this letter from a colleague in Canada:

Dear Brother Still, I am happy to inform you that Mrs. Jackson and her interesting family of children arrived safe in very good health and spirits at my house in St. Catharines, [Ontario]. On Saturday evening last, with sincere pleasure, I provided them with comfortable quarters till this morning, when they left for Toronto.

The Legacy of a Washer Woman
In Toronto the Jacksons crowded at first into a modest clapboard home owned by Thornton and Lucie Blackburn, who had escaped slavery themselves, fleeing Kentucky nearly a quarter-century before. They ranked as pillars of Toronto's black community and often opened their doors or offered help to newly arrived fugitives. The two families lived together only briefly, but all indications are that the Blackburns and the Jacksons enjoyed a long, close friendship in the years that followed.

A quick, happy side note: Do you remember those two older children who had been taken away from Ann and her husband back in Milford and assigned to another Delaware location, the event that sent her husband off the deep end? Both those young men managed to escape slavery as well. Incredibly, both found their family and settled in Toronto.

In Toronto Ann Maria received assistance from the charitable Toronto House of Industry, where staffers described her as "industrious," but in need of help. She was just "five weeks out of slavery" at that point. Eventually, Ann Maria built a career out of washing clothes for white folks. She was still doing laundry at the age of 69 when her health went south. She died at 70, on Jan. 28, 1880, of "dyspepsia."

But her story doesn't end there, because this slave-turned-washerwoman seems to have been a miracle worker of a mother. By all accounts she placed a high maternal priority on schooling for her children, instilling in them a deep regard for the importance of learning.

Consider two examples of what her offspring accomplished in life. Richard "Dirk" Jackson became a barber who managed a pair of shops and catered to a good number of Toronto's political and cultural elite. Ads for "Dick and Rube's" barbershop appear regularly in Toronto's newspapers in the 1870s.

Dirk died young, at age 38 in 1885, of emphysema. His funeral was quite the civic event. This is from a 2008 book titled *I've Got a Home in Glory Land: A Lost Tale of the Underground Railroad*, which touches on the story of the Jacksons while focusing primarily on the lives of the Jacksons' friends, Thornton and Lucie Blackburn:

Half of Toronto's businessmen and a good proportion of the municipal politicians turned out for the funeral of this well-liked young man. The services took place at the St. John's Ward British Methodist Episcopal Church on Chestnut Street on June 2, 1885. Long obituaries appeared in the Toronto World and in the Globe.

One [obituary], on June 3, 1885, in the World, said that "a thousand people were at the funeral, including aldermen and military officers, former mayors of the city, and a host of the town's

*notables [who had] all frequented his shop, ... while Dick deftly
scraped their faces he entertained them with the latest gossip of
the day—political, personal, and social.*

*The newspaper accounts of Jackson's death said that Jackson
"was well liked by both the white and colored population ... Not
a few will miss the deceased from their acquaintanceship." The
procession of more than fifty carriages and hundreds of pedes-
trians wound its way through the city streets from the corner of
Queen Street east of Bay to the Necropolis, which was about half
a mile to the east. Both the publisher of the Toronto World and
John Ross Robertson, of the Toronto Telegram, were in atten-
dance. This was a remarkable tribute to a man whose value to the
community clearly transcended any divisions of race or class that
existed in the highly stratified late-nineteenth-century city.*

As for Albert, he got a menial job with the postal service, then
commenced to slowly but surely climb a career ladder. On May
17, 1882 he earned a promotion that would have made him the
first black man in Canada ever appointed to the position of public
mail carrier.

But the promotion sparked outrage. During his first day
at the new gig Albert's colleagues refused to show him the ropes.
That same day the *Evening Telegram* newspaper ran a piece head-
lined "The objectionable African." The story described him as an
"obnoxious colored man" and referred in an approving tone to the
"intense disgust of the current post office staff" over news of his
promotion.

The postal service backed down immediately, reassign-
ing Jackson to a more menial position. But this turn of events
outraged Toronto's black community. The campaign in support of

Albert Jackson was led by his popular barber brother, the still-living-at-this-time Dirk. Presumably, the prominent Blackburn family chimed in on Albert's behalf as well.

Two days later the *Evening Telegram* backed down, printing an editorial saying,

Objection to the young man on account of his color is indefensible. ... Taxes are not made a penny less to a man because he happens to have dark skin.

The implication there was that government jobs should be available to all tax-paying citizens. In a way Albert got lucky. An important local election was coming up, one that Prime Minister John A. Macdonald really, really wanted his party to win. Worried about losing black votes, he intervened and ordered the postal service to put Albert on the streets as a mail carrier after all.

Albert set out on his route for the first time in early June, and that's what he kept doing in the decades that followed. Jackson got married and had four children. He saved up enough money to buy his family a home in 1914. He died on Jan. 14, 1918.

No one paid much attention to his story until recently. That street in the Harbord Village neighborhood was named after him in 2013. That historical marker went up in downtown Toronto in 2017. That commemorative stamp in his honor was issued in 2019. That mail-sorting facility was named in his honor in 2023.

Personally, I think there is still one bit of unfinished business left when it comes to celebrating the accomplishments of the Jackson family. How about a stamp here in America honoring Ann Maria Jackson?

If I had my way, the words on that stamp would read "Mother of the Century."

11 INTERLUDE
THE TEENAGER'S ROMANTIC INNOVATION

Charles Briddell was an Eastern Shore boy who made good. The wildly successful company that bore his name is known in history books for creating the Carvel Hall Knife—the first utensil ever marketed as a steak knife. You'll find a ton of those vintage collectibles on eBay nowadays.

Briddell wasn't just innovative as a businessman—he also had a creative streak when it came to teenage romance. Growing up in the 1890s along Marumsco Creek—that's well below Marion Station in Somerset County, Md.—he was a farm kid who hated farm fields. All he wanted was to spend all day every day puttering around in the blacksmith shop.

Except for Sundays. Once a teenage Briddell spotted a pretty young thing named Ruth Maddox singing in the choir at Quindocqua United Methodist Church, he commenced traveling seven or eight miles to those services every Sunday, hoping to catch her eye and coax her into his life.

The odds were stacked against him. A whole lot of other boys were chasing Ruth, too. Ruth's first impression:

Charlie seemed bashful and would go home disappointed.

She underestimated that young man. Charles was not one to give up in the face of disappointment. Retreating into his beloved blacksmithing workshop, he emerged one winter Sunday with a made-by-his-own-hand horse-drawn sleigh, gliding oh-so-smoothly along snow-covered roads.

Later, Ruth remembered the sleigh as "bright and shiny." She never forgot the look on Charles's face the day she agreed to climb aboard.

Oh, he was so proud ... as we rode along the snow-covered countryside with the sleigh bells jingling on the horse's neck and the warm lap robe over our knees.

When the weather got warmer Charles took his romantic game to another level. He showed up one spring Sunday riding a shiny new buggy—again built by his own hands. It boasted fancy, then-newfangled rubber tires. And it had another innovation, this one a matter of shape and width. It was unusually narrow across the seating area.

Seeing Charles and Ruth squeezed oh-so-tightly onto that seat inspired Charles's friends to give the buggy a nickname. Ruth never forgot that either:

They used to call it the 'HMT.' That meant 'Hug-Me-Together.'

You know how it ends. Charles and Ruth were married in 1905. They had six children over three-plus decades of marital bliss. Some of those kids inherited the business, and those kids are the ones who brought those early steak knives to market.

12 COURAGE
AN AUTO MECHANIC LEAVES FOOTPRINTS ON THE SANDS OF TIME

In thinking about what the 34-year-old auto mechanic Clarence Spear did on an icy winter's day in January 1920, the logical place to start is with a bit of famous 19th century poetry:

Lives of great men all remind us
We can make our lives sublime,
And, departing, leave behind us
Footprints on the sands of time.

Henry Wadsworth Longfellow wrote that in the 1800s, so he had no idea about Clarence Spear. Neither did I until one of his descendants—a guy named Russell Spear—came across the text of an old newspaper story about the day Clarence played the role of life-saving hero. Russell shared that story on a Facebook page I follow that's devoted to "Cambridge Memories"—as in the Eastern Shore town of Cambridge, Md. Here is the story:

Ordinary Heroes of Old Delmarva

Clarence L. Spear saved Oneita E. Hubbard from drowning
Oneita, 9, broke through thin ice and fell into Cambridge Creek
150 feet from the bank, where the water was 10 feet deep. Spear,
34, [an] automobile mechanic, skated to a point 10 feet from
the hole, lay on the ice, and slid about eight feet; he then broke
through and went slightly under the surface. He rose and took
hold of Oneita, but she crawled upon his shoulders, causing both
to go under the surface twice. Supporting Oneita, Spear trod wa-
ter until a boat was brought over the ice to them, and Oneita was
lifted into it. Spear was drawn up on the ice by a rope.

In looking into this I learned that there was more—much more—
to the story of the miracle Clarence Spear performed that day. Actually, three children had fallen through the ice a way off from the
foot of Muir Street. Apparently, sewage discharge from a nearby
pipe had warmed up the water underneath the ice, weakening it.

After Oneita had climbed up onto his shoulder, Spear
turned his attention to little Mildred Lyons, grabbing hold of her
hair and refusing to let go. Consider: In a frozen creek, Spear
was striving to tread water with one desperate girl draped on his
shoulders and another clutched by the hair. Still, that did not stop
him from going after the third child. He screamed over and over
again for that boy to grab onto his coat and hang on. Sadly, Benjamin Lyons lost his grip and went under. The frenzied scene that
afternoon nearly cascaded into further catastrophe, according to
the Cambridge *Daily Banner*:

While the excitement was at its height, owing to so many crowd-
ing around the place, the ice broke [in additional places], and
quite a number [of other people] were thrown in. They were all
rescued.

'Thank God for People Like Him'
Back to modern times on social media: A woman named Allison
Bramble Marshall happened to see the old story Russell Spear
posted on Facebook, and it blew her mind. She chimed in with
this comment:

*I'm the great-granddaughter of Oneita! She is still living and will
be 106 [years old] this September. I have never heard this story
but thank God for people like him!*

Allison posted a photo of Oneita, showing the centenarian cra-
dling in her arms a great-great-grandchild who never would have
made it into the world if Clarence Spear hadn't played the role of
life saver on Cambridge Creek in 1920.
      This social media stuff all happened a few years back.
I am sorry to report that Oneita passed away in the summer of
2017. Her obituary contains a long list of surviving footprints on
the sands of time: a son, a stepson, a grandson, two step grand-
sons, a step granddaughter, two great granddaughters, four step
great grandchildren, and several great great grandchildren.
      The first time I mentioned this story on the Secrets of the
Eastern Shore website, the focus was on Oneita. But in the years
that followed I heard from Barbara Morris, the granddaughter of
Mildred Lyons. She asked for my help in sharing with modern-
day descendants of Clarence Spear some more footprints left by
Clarence Spear. As she put it:

Everything comes full circle here on the Eastern Shore.

I also heard from Doris Lyons, whose mother-in-law was a sister of Benjamin and Mildred. She relayed a scene of heartbreaking sadness that had been passed down as family lore. Benjamin's father, Oscar Lyons, worked in a nearby shipyard. He had injured one arm at that workplace so badly that it had become permanently useless. Upon hearing that Benjamin was lost and presumed drowned, Oscar got out a pair of oyster tongs and (even with that dead arm) joined in the search for his son's body.

In the days after Mildred was saved and Benjamin lost his life, the family took out an ad in the Cambridge *Banner*:

We desire to publicly express our deepfelt thanks for the many kindnesses shown and offered us during our recent bereavement. We thank those who worked so heroically to save our precious boy and all others who in any way assisted.

Short Life, Long Legacy
As to the life saver, Clarence Spear got his well-deserved 15 minutes of fame. He was awarded a big national Carnegie Hero award for his actions on Cambridge Creek. He died in his late 50s, suffering a heart attack on a February day in 1942 while trying to control a grass fire at his farm in the Neck District outside of Cambridge.

There is one more twist to the story. On the website of the Carnegie Hero Fund (which is still going today) is a story about a granddaughter of Spear's. Shirley Spear Reed of Severn, Md. was born eight years after his death. She had no idea about her granddad's heroics until she grew curious about her family's history as she got older. After finding her way to the website of the Carnegie Hero Fund, she had a bronze marker created to commemorate her grandfather's heroics. That marker is now attached to Spear's gravestone in Dorchester Memorial Park.

Ms. Reed shared a little family oral history on the Carnegie site about the quiet later life of Clarence Spear:

Reed said that in addition to being a mechanic, Spear farmed, growing corn, tomatoes, kale, collard greens, and other crops that he sold to local markets. He once met Annie Oakley, the famous sharpshooter, who showed him her techniques. They were passed down through the family to Reed herself when she learned to shoot as a teenager.

What Clarence Spear did that day in 1920 is amazing in itself. But it gets much more amazing when thinking about how his actions cascaded down through generations that followed. The whole package leaves me with an imagined image: Oneita Mc-Call and Mildred Lyons are chatting up in heaven with Clarence Spear, telling him stories from across many decades about the countless footprints on the sands of time that Spear left behind.

Afternote: That Bit About Annie Oakley
The timing works on that anecdote. Annie Oakley lived in Cambridge for a few years starting in 1912.

13 FORGIVENESS
FROM GRIEF TO GRACE:
A MARYDEL WHODUNNIT

Forgiveness is not weak. It takes courage to face and overcome powerful emotions.
—Desmond Tutu

Every murder is shocking. But some stand out even by the heinous nature of the crime. That's how it felt in the first weeks after Charles Pippin died in January 1909. The setting was so unlikely! Little Marydel, which straddles the Maryland/Delaware border west of Dover, had just 40 homes, a couple of stores, a grist mill, and a cannery. Crime was rare, serious crime unheard of.

An undertaker by trade, Pippin was a "great favorite" in town, "a genial soul, a kind-hearted, helpful, cheerful citizen." Folks loved it when his "sweet, clear" singing voice rang out at church services and camp meetings. They loved the fact that he had recently proposed to a popular young schoolteacher, Maud Hummer. His burial, according to one old newspaper article, drew "the largest number of people, perhaps, ever seen at a Marydel funeral."

Pippin died in a most strange and shocking manner. He

had a starring role in a musical farce titled "The Only Girl," an amateur production that raised funds for the music ministry at his church. He was on stage, in character, snatching a glass of wine from another character and downing it in a big, angry guzzle.

He knew immediately that something was wrong.

"Oh, that burns bad," he improvised, going off script. "Give me some water, quick."

A fellow performer caught on. The water that soon appeared helped, but not much.

Only by manifest pluck and determination [did Pippin] struggle through the play to the end.

By the time he got home Pippin was deathly ill. Someone sent for a specialist. That doctor guessed it was a case of poisoning. Ten bedridden days passed. Then Charles Pippin took his last breath. What happened next:

The little town of Marydel was thrown into an intense state of excitement.

A Poisoned Atmosphere, Full of Rumors and Suspicion
Put this in perspective: Is there somebody like Charles Pippin in your town, your neighborhood? Thinking that way about my home of Cambridge, Md., a couple of faces leap to mind. Both are regulars in local stage productions. Both are blessed with "sweet, clear" singing voices. Both are A-plus citizens and neighbors. If either died in the manner of Charles Pippin, well, I can't even get my head around the volcano of emotions that would

erupt in town.

Coroner W.G. Smith ... declares that the case shall be worked to the finish and that, whoever the guilty parties may be, they shall receive the punishment deserved. That the poison was administered by some person who had a grudge against one of the members of the amateur company is considered certain.

The coroner convened a formal inquest, assembling a jury of local citizens. They agreed on the cause of death, a "poison of some kind unknown." One big-city newspaper writer jumped to the conclusion that the suffocating small-town atmosphere in which the crime unfolded would make it easy to solve.

In a little town like Marydel the likes and dislikes and the petty squabbles and jealousies of nearly every member of the community are public property and there ought not to be any very great difficulty in finding the guilty party and tracing a motive.

It's true that small towns are not always Norman Rockwellish idylls of neighborliness. And it's especially true when it comes to rumors and suspicions around local controversies. The grapevine in Marydel buzzed with theories untethered from facts and evidence. One rumor: One of the other actors must have been the intended victim, as Pippin was beloved by all. Another rumor pointed the finger of blame at Pippin's betrothed, Maud Hummer. The theory? Love gone wrong.

Citizens of [Marydel] are awaiting with anxiety the result of the state chemist's examination of the stage wine.... Since it has been learned that Pippin's sweetheart took a white powder to the theat-

*rical entertainment ... special interest is taken in the examination
of the white sediment in the glass from which Pippin sipped his
doom.*

Can you hear the hushed, all-knowing whispers ricocheting
around the small town? The fact-free explanations, shifting this
way and that while passed from neighbor to neighbor like in a
game of telephone?

*Nearly every member of the [theatrical] company felt a finger of
suspicion was being directed [at them at some point during the
investigation].*

The Culprits Come Clean
Finally, on Jan. 28, news came of a development in the case that
was based on actual facts instead of idle speculation:

*It is stated upon good authority that bichloride of mercury, one
of the most deadly poisons, was found in some of the fluid [exam-
ined by] State Chemist Penniman at Baltimore.*

Finally, State's Attorney Elmer Deen and Detective Pohler—none
of the old newspapers give his first name—had something to go
on. The sale of bichloride of mercury is a crime today, but that
wasn't the case in the early 1900s. It was used as a household
disinfectant and sometimes, as a treatment for syphilis.

Investigators sifted through store records and asked
around about who had purchased the stuff recently. Then they
received an anonymous letter, postmarked from Philadelphia,
suggesting that they take a look at Samuel and Maude Pippin.

Despite the same last name, these Pippins were no relation to the dead man. But they were his friends. They were also involved in the theatrical production. In fact they had delivered the sipped-his-doom concoction. It was supposed to be some sort of raspberry vinegar cocktail. Next the investigators learned that these new Pippins had been in recent possession of bichloride of mercury.

That bottle had gone missing.

The Marydel rumor mill must have been running at warp speed by the time the Pippins sat down with State's Attorney Deen. The couple probably arrived at that session in dread fear of ending up as prime suspects, and that fear seems to have led them astray, as they told a couple of fibs and smudged a couple of facts.

The Pippins had not talked as freely as they should and admitted things only after considerable questioning. In short, [State's Attorney Deen] is not satisfied with their statements.

The Pippins broke down in the end, confessing not to murder but to a horrible accident. Maude thought she had disposed of an empty bottle of bichloride of mercury by tossing it down a well. But she'd thrown away the wrong bottle.

[Once Mrs. Pippin heard that the state chemist had identified the poison, however] she began to fear that the bottle she threw down the well was not her poison bottle and that one of the bottles labeled for the play by her husband must have been the bottle which had formerly contained her corrosive sublimate solution.

Forgiveness Comes in Three Steps
In speaking to the media after her confession Maude Pippin touched on a concept that sounds not so much from the early

1900s, but from our 21st century. Modern-day psychologists, mindfulness teachers, and self-help gurus talk and write often about the importance of self-forgiveness in moving through hard times.

This is a sad hour, when I think of that boy as I last saw him in his casket. I would as soon have given my husband poison as to give it to Charles Pippin. ... Our sorrow is just beginning, and my only consolation is that none of us is infallible.

The state's attorney made some noises about lingering doubts, but he and Detective Pohler couldn't come up with anything approaching a motive. They concluded that the Pippins had told little lies and half-truths not to try and get away with murder, but out of a sense of shame and in fear of being falsely tarred as killers.

So it was an accident.

Still, put yourself in the shoes of the dead man's family, trying to come to terms with the carelessness Maude Pippin had exhibited in tossing the wrong bottle down the well. Imagine how you might feel about someone who tried to cover up a mistake that led to the death of your son. What the Pippins did is akin to a driver's deadly moment of inattention on our modern highways, followed by a clumsy, less than truthful attempt to avoid taking responsibility.

Righteous anger seems a reasonable reaction, doesn't it? Even a more generous soul might make a little wish that the inadvertent killer would long live in an emotional sea of guilt and regret.

But here's the amazing thing about this story: Maude Pippin was wrong in her tearful prediction that the "only consolation" ahead for her and her husband would come through self-forgiveness and accepting that fallibility is an inevitable part of the human condition.

She and Samuel received consolation aplenty from neighbors in their small town. Investigators were probably helped on the road to deciding their innocence by the way people in Marydel reacted to news of the Pippins' confession. One newspaper quoted Rev. E.H. Derrickson of the town's Methodist church:

If you knew the Pippins as I and the better class do here, you would not dare utter a syllable indicating suspicion. ... There is not a man or woman in Caroline [C]ounty more innocent of murdering Charles Pippin in our belief than Brother S.H. Pippin and his wife.

The third bit of forgiveness is the most extraordinary of the bunch. Ironically, the one party in this drama that never fell for any rumor-mill ugliness was the family of the late Charles Pippin. The day after his brother died, H.W. Pippin of Elkton was quoted predicting that it would turn out to be a case of "unintentional poisoning."

Maude and Samuel Pippin made a public pilgrimage to seek forgiveness from the family of the victim. Newspaper reporters gathered to watch the scene unfold.

There was no hesitation on the part of the victim's family to assure Mrs. Maude Pippin that they realized the young man's death was an accident. So, with tears streaming down their cheeks and embracing each other, two women [Maude and the victim's mother] tried to console each other. For a time it seemed that one or both of the women might collapse, but finally, they became comparatively composed.

Another heart-wrenching scene unfolded when Samuel Pippin stepped forward to greet the father of the dead man.

The old father fell on [Samuel Pippin's] neck, and both cried.

And then, slowly but surely, life in little Marydel returned to normal.

There has been a great deal of excitement for several weeks in our usually quiet little town. There have been a number of newspaper writers here from the cities of Baltimore and Philadelphia and many lengthy press messages, amounting to thousands of words, have been telegraphed from our railroad office. Now the place is resuming its wonted serenity, but the deep and settled sorrow for the sad accident remains and will be felt for many a day hereabout.

In her song "Under the Water," the modern-day pop singer Jewel has a lyrical couplet that seems an appropriate conclusion here:

And there's a tiny light, a flicker within
Forgiveness is the needle that knows how to mend.

Postscript: Time Marches On
Samuel and Maude Pippin moved out of Marydel a few years after this incident, relocating to Wilmington, Del. But they retained strong ties to their old hometown. In the decades that followed the society pages of Caroline County newspapers had frequent little reports about how the Pippins returned to visit friends and

relations. In 1939 the *Wilmington News Journal* did a story about a big party that marked their 50th wedding anniversary.

The victim's fiancée, Maud Hummer, never married. Those society pages reported on her activities often through the years, mentioning trips she took and guests who called at her Marydel home. She was a schoolteacher at the time of Charles Pippin's death, and that's what she remained. She had a 52-year career in the Caroline County schools. She died in 1955 at age 72. Her obituary made no mention of the man to whom she had once been betrothed.

14 GOOD SAMARITAN
FIGHTING THE DEVIL IN ACCOMACK COUNTY

Heroes can be horrible role models sometimes. What, I'm supposed to try and wield a sword like Achilles? Wield a pen like Dostoevsky? Wield compassion like Mother Teresa?

Yeah, right—don't think I'm gonna hit those targets.

This problem can be quite acute here on my home turf of Maryland's Eastern Shore, where the heroes of slavery times are celebrated at every turn. The most famous names here are Harriet Tubman and Frederick Douglass. Both were born into slavery, and both rose to unfathomable heroic heights by taking insane risks and racking up miraculous accomplishments. Hundreds of other, lesser-known "conductors" and "station masters" hereabouts put everything on the line—family, freedom, their lives—to pitch in by helping people escape from bondage.

They're all heroes of the first order, but role models? What chance do my little modern-day feet have of fitting comfortably into their gargantuan, world-changing shoes? I suspect this is why I was so struck by some stories of slavery times told by Rev. Adam Wallace, a contemporary of those heroes. He was a white man who opposed slavery, but he never took the dive into the deep end of the movement. He did smaller, simpler things. He may not have changed the world, but he helped Uncle Sammy.

On the Road to Locustville

In 1854 the Methodist powers that be assigned Wallace to a circuit of several congregations on the Eastern Shore of Virginia. Today the drive from his old assignment in Lewes, Del. to his new one in Locustville, Va. would be a simple two-hour affair. It took Wallace 10 days to make that journey with his family and two wagons of belongings.

Times were different. But if you've ever wandered the backroads of Virginia's Eastern Shore, you know the place is blessed with landscapes that have a magically timeless quality. So it is with the blink-and-miss-it crossroads of Locustville. Drive through today and you'll see one building that started life as a general store in 1884 and another that served stagecoach passengers as the Locustville Hotel in the 1820s. The Victorian-style Locustville Academy, which opened in 1859, still stands, too. Historian Kirk Mariner once described modern-day Locustville as the closest thing left to the way things looked on Virginia's Eastern Shore before the Civil War.

The town is a few miles south of Accomac, the seat of Accomack County. The road through it is called Drummondtown Road because that's what Accomac was called in Wallace's time. After moving his family into an old carriage shop that had been repurposed into a parsonage, Wallace set about getting to know the place. He sensed straight away an "extreme sensitiveness" among the faithful when it came to the issue of slavery.

In official teaching the Methodist Church in those years landed mostly on the anti-slavery side of the aisle. But ministers in communities where pro-slavery sentiments ran strong tended to approach the issue with something more like a live-and-let-live mushiness. Slave owners went to church secure in the knowledge they would not be harangued from the pulpit. Slaves were either unwelcome or relegated to the balcony.

Wallace is quite honest in his memoirs about the fact that he never signed on with the "rabid stripe" of abolitionism. He didn't drop everything to fight the injustice of it all. He tried to make a difference in smaller ways, by treating the individuals who crossed his path with dignity and respect.

'We Had a Precious Time with the Saints'
Wallace took one step in this direction on his first Sunday in Locustville. The way things worked before his arrival: White people on the main floor came up front to receive communion at a rail. Then, as if in an afterthought, a bowl of sacred hosts got shuttled up to the balcony and passed around among black folks. The idea was that the main floor of the church, and especially its sacred communion rail, shouldn't be sullied by blackness.

After serving communion at the rail to the main floor white folks, Wallace paused and "made a brief address, saying that at this one point [of holy communion], all social distinction must vanish." To do otherwise, he preached, would "dishonor Christ." Then he invited the black worshippers to climb down from the balcony and gather at the communion rail.

Half of the white folks walked out in disbelief at this offense to their sensibilities. Wallace let them go, focusing instead on the souls who stepped up to the rail.

Meanwhile, we [had] a precious time with the old saints around the altar. They apprehended a present Christ and, with tears of

*joy and exclamations of love and praise, they [stood at the rail
and] celebrated the great fact of their salvation.*

After the service some sympathetic white folks whispered to Wallace that threats were being made against him. Those folks who walked out were plotting to round up some ruffians to escort the new preacher out of town. Instead, the controversy blew over, thanks in part to the way a bigwig bishop named Levi Scott gave the revamped communion service his public blessing.

'A Piece of Injustice and Indignity'
The next step Wallace took along these lines landed him in a mess. He and his wife were riding a carriage through the countryside at Christmastime. Approaching a store they came upon two white men using rope to bind the hands and feet of a "venerable colored man." Wallace thought they were treating that man too roughly, especially when one of the white guys pressed his knee onto the breast of an "unresisting, heartbroken slave."

Wallace "leapt" from his carriage and commenced castigating the men. He threw out the words "cowardly maltreatment." One of the men warned the preacher to mind his own business.

*I replied [that] it was my business always and everywhere to fight
the devil.*

The men rode off, that venerable colored man in tow. Several people who had gathered outside the store witnessed the scene. From them Wallace learned the black man's name, Uncle Sammy. He learned, too, that Uncle Sammy had been freed 10 years before by his master, a man who had since passed away. He learned that Sammy had built a cabin he shared with his wife and family.

111

He learned that Sammy had been a "diligent workman" while toiling as a "sawyer" to prepare the lumber used during construction of one of the churches on Wallace's circuit.

He asked those strangers about the white guys. One had married the widow of Sammy's former owner. The other had married that owner's daughter. Both were heavy drinkers and frequent gamblers. The theory in the crowd outside the store was that "both had probably been on a spree and run out of money." Now they were kidnapping Sammy, planning to sell him and replenish their pockets. Most likely the pair would then "drink and gamble away" whatever price the old man fetched.

Wallace asked for volunteers to help him stand up for Sammy, but there were no takers in the crowd. Everyone was too scared of the kidnappers. One guy advised Wallace to gather up his family and leave Virginia immediately.

They said ... nobody cares to have a row with such desperate characters. [They said those men] would knife a man in a jiffy, and they added it was a mercy [one of them] had not knifed me.

But Wallace could not let things stand.

No, my Irish was up ... If such a piece of injustice and iniquity were allowed to go unchallenged, I could not live or preach in such a place under the gathering frowns of Almighty God.

He dropped his wife off at the carriage-shop-cum-parsonage and rode to Drummondtown, where slave sales happened. Upon arrival he learned that the white guys had sold Sammy for $300. Sammy wasn't gone yet, however. He was parked in a cell in the county jail. That's where he would sit until enough slaves

112

had gathered to make up a full "gang" for transport toward new homes across the Chesapeake Bay, in points south.

Wallace wandered through town, trying to find a lawyer who would help him file "some sort of writ" to put Sammy's situation before judges in a courtroom. He got a string of refusals, but then "a farmer who used to be a lawyer" stepped up and said he'd write something up.

That's how Sammy got his day in court. His prospects seemed bleak at first. The chief judge on the panel that heard the case was rich, prominent, and very unpopular. He'd earned his fortune "as a sort of hustler," by being "shrewd at cards" and running scams. Local townsfolk "despised" this judge "for his origins and flagrant immoralities."

In a surprise, however, this greedy hustler took Sammy's side in the case. He launched into "a fine philippic on the rascality of taking a freed man and selling him in his declining years for a paltry $300." He told his fellow judges to think about how Sammy's former owner had freed Sammy before dying. He asked them to think about their own "property" holdings and to imagine no-good relatives ignoring provisions in their wills.

Suppose ... after we are in our graves some irresponsible vagabonds should assume to trample on our wishes.

The court freed Uncle Sammy. Better yet, they ordered the arrest of the two white men who'd kidnapped him. Those two men never came to trial. Upon hearing of the judges' decision,

[They] harnessed their horses and left Drummondtown at a tearing gallop, to be seen or heard of no more, at least while I was in Virginia.

113

The next Sunday Wallace climbed the pulpit at Garrison's Chapel in the town of Painter—the church went up in 1855 and still stands today. As Wallace looked out at the faithful gathered before him, he saw a glorious sight:

Uncle Sammy, his face all wet with rolling tears of gratitude.

Wallace lived until 1903. A thoughtful man, he must have recognized in his later years that his contributions to the cause of human dignity in slavery times were minuscule compared with other, bigger heroes of freedom on the Delmarva Peninsula and around the country. Did that comparison leave him feeling like a failure? I don't think so, at least judging by the words on the front cover of the autobiography published shortly after his death. The words he chose to sum up his life were the ones he spoke on the day he happened upon that "venerable old black man" in distress: *My Business Was to Fight the Devil.* Here's hoping you and I manage to earn in our modern days a measure of the pride Wallace felt in extending a helping hand to a neighbor in need.

15 COMMUNITY
MAY ROE ROBERTS: A
TROOPER IN SUDLERSVILLE

Every little Delmarva town has its heroes. Some fight fires. Some tackle crime. Some build businesses and create jobs. Others, like May Roe Roberts, start Girl Scout troops.

That might not seem like a big deal, but stick with me. Learning about May Roberts brought my late mother to mind. She was around 80 when my wife and I set out to do a little family-history booklet. Mom shared memories with us during those days, none more vivid than her recollection of an inspiring and hyper-dedicated gym teacher named Irma J. Thorpe. Mom's eyes lit up with unbridled joy as she recalled raucous, demanding after-school sessions of dodgeball and gymnastics.

That didn't exactly fit my preconceptions about what schoolgirl life was like back in the 1930s. The girls of Sudlersville, on Maryland's Upper Eastern Shore, had it even better than my mom in those years.

Roberts first stepped into the Girl Scout game in the summer of 1926, which makes her pretty close to a scouting pioneer. Juliette Gordon Low formed the first troop in the country in Savannah, Georgia just 15 years before that. Most troops in those

115

early days were in big cities, not middle-of-nowhere farm towns.

Roberts was 44 years old at this point, a housewife with three daughters and a son. The Sudlersville native had come of age in ways that were unusual for a woman born in 1885. She'd graduated from high school, something less than 10 percent of Americans (women *and* men) did as the 1900s dawned. She'd gone further, finishing college. Along the way she'd learned to love competing on basketball and tennis courts.

The newspaper articles and historical essays I reviewed about Roberts don't pinpoint what inspired her to jump into the Girl Scout game. Perhaps she felt little Sudlersville didn't offer her girls the opportunities she'd enjoyed in her younger days. Perhaps she simply discovered along life's way that working with young people brought her joy.

What we know for sure is that she made that jump with both feet. Roberts marched all over town in 1926 and 1927, recruiting girls to become scouts. She eventually got a dozen takers, including her daughters Helen and Martha. Her youngest, Anna, would come aboard when she got a little older.

'We Did All of the Things Gypsies Do'
One legend that lingers today around Sudlersville is that Roberts started the first-ever Girl Scout troop on the Delmarva Peninsula. In a historical essay about scouting on Delmarva Pat Bjorke confirms that Roberts did indeed "begin the legacy of Girl Scouts on the Eastern Shore of Maryland and Virginia." Her group of Sudlersville girls went by the name "Girl Scout Troop #1" back in the day.

Roberts decided early on that she should be on friendly terms with her girls. She ordered them to stop calling her Mrs. Roberts.

It didn't sound like there was enough feeling between us, so I came up with "Robbie."

In those early years Robbie often showed up for meetings on horseback. She sewed uniforms for her charges by hand. Like many troop leaders in those days she focused some on cooking, cleaning, and home economics skills. But Robbie was determined to push her girls in other directions, too. She talked a local blacksmith into making a couple of basketball hoops. She led the girls on ice skating, hiking, and canoeing expeditions. One craft project involved transforming old inner tubes into toys. Another had the girls refurbishing their own tattered old toys and delivering the rebuilt playthings to shelters and orphanages. A message she tried to deliver at every turn:

If you can mount one obstacle, you can mount another.

Robbie's biggest claim to Girl Scout fame lay in the way she helped her girls discover the broader world. The term Robbie used to describe their travels is "gypsy trips," because

We slept on the ground and did all of the things gypsies do.

Here are a few of the destinations the girls of Sudlersville explored starting in the late 1920s: the Shenandoah Valley in Virginia, the mountains of Vermont, Niagara Falls, Fort Ticonderoga in New York, Plymouth Rock in Massachusetts, the World's Fair in New York City, the Kitty Hawk airfield in North Carolina, and our nation's capital in Washington, D.C.

They traveled on one occasion to a Kentucky horse farm

to visit an aging racing legend, Man o' War. Robbie said later that the history of this visit was recorded on the farm's visitor log books. She and the girls were among the last visitors to see Man o' War before he died.

He was a perfectly gorgeous horse. He put his head right on my shoulder and nestled up to me.

The biggest trip of all had the girls venturing well north of Toronto to Callander, Ontario for a visit with the "Dionne quintuplets." The healthy birth of those kids in 1934 had set off an international media sensation—it was the first time five quintuplets had all survived early infancy.

These excursions were not luxury affairs. There weren't any big donors or fancy accommodations involved. Mostly, the girls camped out in tents. Sometimes they slept in barns. They built fires to cook their meals. One old newspaper story offered a hint as to just how out-of-the-ordinary this was in the scouting world:

As far as [Robbie] knows her Sudlersville troop was the first in the United States to go "trip camping."

They'd rent a bus and hire a driver. The girls climbed aboard carrying duffel bags they'd made themselves out of feed bags and dyed green. They'd pack the bus with tents, foodstuffs, and cooking gear. Robbie wasn't shy in her trip planning. She would write to or telephone strangers who owned land along the way, explaining what was up and winning permission to camp on their land or take over a barn. She somehow talked the Esso oil company into preparing trip maps with customized routes carefully highlighted.

During one trip the girls got pulled over by a cop on a New York highway. That cop said the bus interior was too over-loaded, to the point of being unsafe.

[The] girls immediately unloaded all their gear and lashed it to the top of the bus in order to complete their trip.

Here is what Robbie had to say about the cost of these trips:

When we went to Canada we traveled 2,370 miles and the cost [per Girl Scout] per day was just a little over $1. We were poor in one way, but not in another. ... We'd pile in a bus and take off. We'd sleep wherever we were.

'In Case Those Boys from Centreville [Get] Up to No Good'
There was lots more fun. Robbie used to swing free tickets to Navy football games, followed by free admittance to fancy-schmancy post-game dances where the girls would swoon in delight watching handsome young cadets, though always "under the eagle eye of Mrs. Roberts and her chaperones."

As the years went on Robbie became famous as a scout-ing advocate all over the region. She would often set out along the rural back roads through Delaware, Maryland, or Virginia in response to a request to help get a troop started in this, that, or another small town. Pat Bjorke again:

No one can say precisely how many [troops] she started.

During the 1930s she sweet-talked landowners at Bookers Wharf on the Chester River near Centreville into letting her set up a summer camp for Girl Scouts on their property. Soon, troops from all over Delmarva were overnighting in the wild at "Camp Chester." This quote about life in the early days of that camp might make you laugh out loud:

Ever watchful and protecting of her girls, Captain Roberts would sleep in a tent by the road with a shotgun, "just in case those boys from Centreville decided to be up to no good."

One of the newspaper articles I reviewed here was published in 1965, shortly after Robbie had turned 80 years old. A widow by this point, she celebrated that big round birthday by going for a little stroll to visit one of her former Girl Scout charges. The route covered 10 miles. A few words from the gospel according to Robbie:

I really and truly have had a wonderful life. But you know, you have to make your wonderful life. It won't come to you naturally. Nope. I've conquered a great many things.

The reporter who worked up that article asked Robbie at one point about a fancy buckle on the belt that circled her waist. Apparently, that was a keepsake from her younger days as a single girl.

That buckle is an old boyfriend's, honey. I took it from one of my Naval Academy beaus. You see, I'm not as "good" as you might think I am.

Robbie put in four-plus decades as a scout leader in Sudlersville and a scouting inspiration across Delmarva. She passed away in 1970 at age 87. She's resting today in the Sudlersville Cemetery.

I wonder: How many of her girls shared memories much later in life with children and grandchildren of their adventures with Robbie? Did their eyes shine with the same joy my elderly mother felt recalling her favorite gym teacher? That right there— well, it's God's work.

16 COMMUNITY
'IT'S A WONDERFUL LIFE' ON VIRGINIA'S EASTERN SHORE

Have you ever been sure that prosperity was just around the corner? Perhaps you took a new job or trained for a hot new career path or started your own business. Alas, the riches never came. The worst part: It wasn't your fault. You ended up playing a business game that was rigged against the little guys.

Farmers on Virginia's Eastern Shore were giddy about their prospects back in the 1880s. Pretty much all the experts predicted that a pot of gold lay just beyond the horizon. The railroad was coming at last. Steamboat lines were expanding like crazy. Both would give farmers faster, more reliable access to big-city markets like Baltimore, Philadelphia, and even New York.

Think of all the money to be made! Many farm families switched things up to pave a path toward that prosperity, transitioning from old staples like corn and oats into more perishable products—cabbage, onions, berries, and potatoes.

But the pot of gold turned out to be a mirage. Sure, produce got to big cities faster, before spoiling. The problem came after that, when berries and potatoes disappeared into a black hole of big-city businesses practices that were messy, complicated, and sometimes pretty shady.

More often than not, the cash that came back out of that big-city black hole didn't even cover a farm family's expenses, much less put food on the table. Jacob L. Maxton of Virginia Tech University wrote a dissertation in the 1920s that focused in part on this period of high agricultural hopes amid transportation advances. Here is his bleak bottom line on what happened:

Each year brought its quota of [farm] bankruptcies.

What chance did these farmers have? Most had little education, perhaps a few years of grade school. They didn't have money for lawyers and accountants. There was no Better Business Bureau to call. Heck, they didn't even have telephones.

I wouldn't blame them if they'd played the victim card, wallowing in the notion that the world was out to get them.

But that's not what they did. They responded with a we're-all-in-this-together brand of resilience and ingenuity. Remember the Frank Capra film classic, "It's a Wonderful Life?" How George Bailey convinced his neighbors in little Bedford Falls to bet their life savings on his plan to launch a banking cooperative as a fair-and-square alternative to the old-school bank owned by greedy, heartless Mr. Potter?

That's pretty much what happened here, only the ending was even better. As the credits roll on "It's a Wonderful Life," Bailey Building & Loan has just survived a financial squeeze through an outpouring of generosity from "little people" in Bedford Falls and beyond. That promises better days ahead, but all that prosperity is left to the imagination of viewers.

We don't need to imagine what the Eastern Shore Produce Exchange accomplished. Remember how farms were going bankrupt left and right in the 1880s? Fast forward a few decades. Here is from a 2006 report by the Virginia Department of Humanities:

• In 1910 Accomack County had the "highest per capita income of any rural county in the United States."

• By the early 1920s the combined region of Accomack and Northampton counties had the "highest crop value per acre of any farm region in the country."

Yup, the Eastern Shore yokels got together and outsmarted the city slickers. How'd they do it? I had great fun digging into those details. I hope you do too.

A Peek Inside That Black Hole

Back to the 1880s. Here, in a few short bullet points, is what happened when farmers on Virginia's peninsula started chasing that transportation-revolution pot of gold.

• The farmers shipped their goods on "consignment." In this context that meant shipping produce from a wharf or rail station without knowing what price it might fetch.

• Where should they send their produce? Philly? Wilmington? Baltimore? To answer that question, they needed to know which cities had a glut of potatoes (driving prices down) and which had a shortfall (bringing prices up). No telephones, remember? There were telegraph lines, but these family farmers didn't have the time or the connections to travel to a telegraph office and spend hours on market research.

• A third problem arose at the big-city "commission houses" that acted as middlemen for rural produce. Sales agents there were paid in a way that gave them no incentive to haggle for higher prices during auctions. Consider potatoes, sold by the barrel. Those middlemen got 10 cents for every barrel sold, no matter the price. They had no reason to fight for some faraway farmer they'd never met.

• Then came delivery. Let's say it's to a grocery store. When the manager there unloaded goods, he often awarded his store generous discounts for spoilage, shortfalls, underweight packages, and other supposed problems. From hundreds of miles away, Eastern Shore farmers had no way to look over the shoulders of those managers and argue about whether those discounts were bogus.

The farmers were screwed. The world kinda *was* out to get them. Lucky families covered expenses and put food on the table. Unlucky ones, well, that explains all those bankruptcies.

A Plan to Turn the Tables
Perhaps my favorite aspect of this story is the way it lacks a singular hero. There was no George Baileyesque savior leading the charge. Dozens of names pop up in old newspaper articles and historical accounts of how the Eastern Shore Produce Exchange succeeded. It was a true communal endeavor, hundreds of people putting heads together, developing a plan, and then betting a big chunk of their meager cash on its results.

Remember the scenes early on in "It's a Wonderful Life" where the "little" people of Bedford Falls are crowded into a big room, debating back and forth about how awful things are and what might be done about it? On the Eastern Shore of Virginia, the first of those meetings convened in the town of Keller on the afternoon on Sept. 9, 1899.

The session was convened in the name of an elder statesman of the farming community, William L. Elzey. He lived along Seaside Road between Exmore and Nassawadox. Among the key people on the 12-member committee that emerged from that meeting were A. J. McMath, Benjamin T. Gunter, and G. Walter Mapp.

That committee soon came up with a recommendation: They proposed establishing a cooperative "marketing organization" that would take over advertising, sales, and delivery of products. Committee members unveiled this plan at a series of "mass meetings" held up and down the Virginia peninsula. Funding would come from farmers who invested in the co-op to the tune of $5, becoming "members." Early on they were allowed to put 25 cents down and pay the rest later.

In a chapter devoted to the exchange in his 1915 business-advice book, *How Farmers Co-operate and Double Profits*, Clarence Poe had a blunt explanation for why so many farmers took a chance on this newfangled idea:

The organization was born out of poverty and disappointments.

The Eastern Shore Produce Exchange launched operations in the spring of 1900. The system they soon got up and running looked like this:

• Commitment to excellence. The produce exchange launched a flagship "brand," Red Star, then set up a system of pre-shipment inspections to guarantee that Red Star products would always be top of the line. They wanted customers to be 100 percent confident in the product.

• A network of sales agents. The produce exchange cut those big-city middlemen out of their business dealings. Instead, they hired their own network of sales agents, structuring their pay so they would be highly motivated to go after the highest price possible.

• No more commission sales. The produce exchange shipped member produce in a fashion known as "F.O.B.," which meant that customers committed themselves to a price before products left a dock or railyard in Virginia.

• A communications network. Using the telegraph at first and later the telephone, the produce exchange hired researchers to track prices and supply levels on a daily basis in various cities. That way, they could make shipping-destination decisions based on where demand and prices were highest.

• A commitment to innovation, on numerous fronts. One example: Trying to establish a bigger market for lower-quality potatoes that didn't meet the Red Star standard of excellence, the produce exchange created advertisements that built consumer demand for potato chips, potato salads, and sweet potato custards. Second example: The produce exchange worked with members to introduce crop varieties that matured on slightly different schedules, thereby extending the harvest sales season beyond a one-fell-swoop week or two. Third example: In the 1920s the produce exchange launched a subsidiary, the Exchange Supply Company, to give members better prices and quality on supplies like fertilizer and containers.

Launching A Farming Revolution

We started here with talk of a transportation revolution, but the Eastern Shore Produce Exchange didn't just pave a road through that transition toward the pot of gold on the horizon. The organization helped spark a mini-revolution in American agriculture.

Early on, these Virginia farmers were in uncharted waters. West Coast farmers set up a California Fruit Growers Exchange in this same time frame, but a good number of historians still rate the Eastern Shore Produce Exchange as a groundbreaking operation.

Writing in the *Peninsula Enterprise* from the post-success vantage point of 1931, Gordy Williams put it this way:

This organization was established almost without precedent, and its early days were fraught with difficulties. ... No warning of the many pitfalls that would beset their path was given, and no financial assistance from the government was solicited. They were pioneers, but they had faith in their organization and persevered, largely blazing their own trail, and they were destined to revolutionize the marketing of farm products.

A similar conclusion appears in a 1961 article published (without attribution to a specific author) in an Eastern Shore of Virginia history project run by the University of Virginia and called "The Countryside Transformed."

The Eastern Shore of Virginia Produce Exchange was the pioneer farmers' cooperative marketing organization in the nation, and its plan of operation became a model for later cooperative marketing organizations in the United States.

Finally, a key conclusion from that previously mentioned 1926 dissertation by Jacob Maxton:

From a small concern whose enemies predicted its failure year by year, [the Eastern Shore Produce Exchange] has reached a pinnacle well above that attained by any other co-operative produce marketing concern in the United States.

In time the organization set up departments dedicated to sales, research, advertising, education, claims, and grower services. The exchange expanded its market reach beyond the East Coast, into the Midwest, up into Canada, and over to Cuba. The exchange had seasonal, salaried employees working to sell Eastern Shore produce in Boston, Providence, Buffalo, Cleveland, Montreal, Toronto, Detroit, Chicago, Cincinnati, Scranton, and elsewhere.

Let's not forget the kind of people who created this amazing success story. The Eastern Shore of Virginia had its share of prominent families that sent children off to college, to be sure, but that was not a path available to the general population of farming families. Virginia didn't establish public schooling until 1869. In those first early decades only one-third to one-half of the state's children were enrolled. A much, much smaller number made it to high school graduation.

And yet, as early as 1902, the *Baltimore Sun* was using these words to describe an annual meeting of exchange members:

A happier and more enterprising body of farmers has seldom been gathered together on the peninsula.

The aforementioned writer Clarence Poe has a humorous note in his book that gets at how prominent the Eastern Shore of Virginia

Produce Exchange was in the early 1900s. Poe recalls a research trip to Onley when he was accompanied by a colleague named Professor W.R. Camp:

"I reckon that's the courthouse," said Professor Camp to me as we walked through the little town ... and came in sight of the handsomest building in the place. But it wasn't the courthouse at all. It was the home office of the Eastern Shore of Virginia Produce Exchange, as a large sign across the front quickly informed us.

The produce exchange continued into the 1950s. I have not come across a detailed explanation of the circumstances of its demise, but that 1961 article published by the University of Virginia shortly after the exchange shut down summed up the bottom line like this:

[D]uring the fifty-five years of its existence [the Eastern Shore Produce Exchange] returned to the farmers of the Shore probably more than a quarter of a billion dollars.

Not bad for a bunch of uneducated yokels up against long odds. Let's try and remember their example the next time it feels like the world is against us.

Afternote #1: A Major Exchange Failure
For all its success and innovation, the Eastern Shore of Virginia Produce Exchange failed to rise above the racial prejudice of its times. Black farmers were not allowed to become full official members of the exchange. They could ship their produce through the exchange, accessing some of its benefits, only by using a sort

of "guest-access" arrangement and paying a yearly fee. They were not allowed to become shareholding owners on an equal standing with white farmers, and as a result, they did not earn the stock dividends that went to shareholding white farmers.

Afternote #2: The Daily Operations

Below is a detailed account of the day-to-day workings of the produce exchange from the 1915 book, *How Farmers Co-operate and Double Profits*. To me, it calls to mind the title of a modern-day business advice book by consultant Marie Forleo: *It's All Figureoutable!*

In order to explain more readily the Exchange's method, let us describe a typical day's work in the shipping season. The first thing the officers do is to phone the Exchange's forty-three [local] agents, the men employed to represent at forty-three shipping points scattered all over the two counties and find out just how many [railroad] cars will be offered for shipment.

Oak Hall, say, will report three cars "[Red] Star brand," Tasley one or two unbranded, Onley five cars "[Red] Star" and so on. Then the totals are footed up, and it is up to the Exchange to sell them for the growers. By 8 or 9 o'clock telegrams report the prevailing New York prices and New York prices, of course, determine prices in a considerable area around New York.

If New York prices are low, then the Exchange may wire its agents in Chicago, Pittsburgh, Toronto, [Boston], and Scranton, and the Exchange officials will also wire as many jobbers in other cities as the size of the day's business seems to require. Perhaps the telegram will read: 'We offer you today one car Red Star $2 barrel.' Perhaps a number of orders will be wired back at this price, but some jobbers will reply: "Cannot pay $2 here but *will take two cars at one ninety."*

By 1 or 2 o'clock the Exchange officials have wired directions for shipping most of the cars, and they also know whether or not all the cars can be sold at the $2 rate. If all cannot be sold at this figure, some orders may be filled at $1.90, or perhaps some may have to be sold at $1.85, in markets where local conditions will not justify the higher price.

Nevertheless, it would be manifestly unfair to pay one farmer $1.85 and another $2, when both had brought to Exchange officials the same grade of potatoes and at the same time. Therefore, it is the custom of the Exchange to pool prices or to average them so that on each day's shipment all farmers will get the same price for the same grade of product.

17 INTERLUDE
'THE INNATE GOODNESS OF THE CREEK FOLKS'

Here, take this and fix it up fer Fred.

That simple run of words speaks to the neighborly ways that characterized life in a small, isolated community of watermen families living and working on the edge of Tangier Sound back in the early 1900s. The quote, uttered by a man named Uncle Ike, appears in *God, Man, Salt Water and the Eastern Shore*, a 1967 memoir by William A. Tawes.

Tawes grew up at the southernmost tip of Somerset County, Maryland, in a community he refers to as "The Creek," after nearby Cedar Island Creek. He starts that book out by talking about the food of his childhood years. From our vantage point in the 21st century, it's easy to imagine places like The Creek were chock full of fresh-caught fish, succulent soft shells, home-grown produce, and sweet baked goods.

Not so much.

The delicacies we associate with Delmarva history—

oysters, crabs, rockfish—were too valuable as commodities back then. The good stuff was reserved for the marketplace of shops and restaurants in nearby towns and distant big cities. Creek folks ate black-eyed peas, navy beans, pork saltside, and a cheap bread called playcake.

Oysters, crabs, rockfish and other creatures of the sea were the gold of the deep and were seldom used in the daily menu. The Creek folks nearly without exception began their day with black coffee and playcake. Milk, much less cream, was only for the sick, but most of the folks used sugar in their coffee. Also, blackstrap molasses was occasionally used in which to sop their playcake or cornpone.

I have never heard of playcake outside of my home community, but I feel it was not entirely original with my people. Playcake was like charity: vaunteth not itself, was not puffed up, and was kind; it satisfied the pangs of hunger when the cupboard was otherwise bare.

It was a simple thing, flour mixed with shortening and a smidge of yeast powder and then "spread out flat in a pan and baked until brown."

It was of relative virtue; it could be as rich as pie crust, or just plain hardtack, which it usually was, and as hard as cement when cold.

When Creek people had fish for supper, it was croaker stew, cooked in a kettle with a cup of water and some green onions. When they had crabs, it was buckram pie, buckram being the name for crabs that had entered a biological stage where they were too hard to pack aboard buyboats bound for packing houses. When bivalves made an appearance on the menu, they were clams, not oysters.

The Creek crabber never brought [softshell crabs] home. They were the finny gold of the shoals and much too valuable to be eaten by their families.

The exception to these rules of Creek living came into play when sickness visited a local family. Tawes himself was bedridden with scarlet fever at a young age. A neighbor came by and gave his mother a diamondback terrapin, which then ranked as a supreme big-city delicacy.

There was a belief in the community that no other food had the healing virtue of broth made from the diamondback. ... Only now, while I am recalling the incident, do I fully appreciate the gift. The bull was worth a dollar for every inch of his belly plate.

Another incident of illness in the Tawes household brings us that quote we started with:

I was home when Uncle Ike stopped by when Father was ill and gave Mother a large rockfish he had caught. "Here, take this and fix it up fer Fred," he said. "It ought to do some good." The fish was large enough for the whole family's supper.

Tawes finishes this piece of his memoir by putting this neighborliness and generosity in a broader, faith-filled perspective:

Uncle Ike went home to his playcake and beans, joying in his act of Christian charity with all of its Biblical implications. The Creek folks detested [receiving] charity in any form. But gifts to the sick person, [that] was another matter; it was ... a Christian gesture of sympathy in time of trouble. In a true sense the food [that neighbors brought by in times of illness] was manna from heaven, inspired by the innate goodness of the Creek folks.

18 TRUE GRIT
STORM OF '39: 'THIS LIFE IS WORTH FIGHTING FOR'

Nothing in the forecast for Feb. 3, 1939 hinted at trouble on the Chesapeake Bay. The *Baltimore Sun* promised a ho-hum winter day: "Rain today, and probably tomorrow. Colder tonight." Oystermen in the Chesapeake Bay didn't see red flags during their workday. A pair of then-young watermen, Art Daniels and Jimmy Murphy, were aboard the *Robert L. Tawes* out of Deal Island, Md. Years later they remembered toiling atop an oyster bar called Under the Cliffs through a "light drizzle" while getting pushed along by a "nice breeze."

They called it a day in mid-afternoon. Under the Cliffs is on the western-shore side of the Bay, near the town of Solomons. Sailing back toward Deal on the Eastern Shore, the *Tawes* had 100 freshly dredged bushels on deck. Another 150 bushels were down in the hold—the previous day's harvest, which they hadn't sold yet.

Many watermen have said through the years that one of the joys in their profession is the way that Mother Nature delivers so many surprises. The quotes you'll come across in books and newspaper articles are some variation of this:

Every day I see something out there I've never seen before.

The words are usually spoken with a sense of wonder and gratitude, but the surprise Mother Nature delivered on that February
day is the deadly flip side of that. The sky above the western
shore cliffs went "black as tar" in the blink of an eye. The crew
on the *Tawes* raced to lower the jib, but ran out of time with the
mainsail. It was still halfway up when the storm hit. No one had
time to measure the speed of the wind. Later, Daniels guesstimated it at 65 miles per hour.

Bringing the boat up into the wind was like hitting a wall.

Murphy always remembered it as the "hardest blow I've ever
seen come across the water." The crew threw two anchors, trying
to stabilize the *Tawes* and keep her upright. Those anchors might
have helped, but in the years that followed Daniels would share
another theory about what saved him and his shipmates. Those
unsold 150 bushels in the hold served as ballast. Six or so other
boats were working Under the Cliffs that day. Each crew probably
had its own tale—superior seamanship there, miraculous good
fortune here, or maybe a little of both. They all stayed afloat.

Trouble on the Choptank
As things turned out, those boats out on the open Bay had survived only the "easy bit" of the "hardest blow." Watermen working inside the Choptank River were about to get the worst of it.

No one had radios. Those open-Bay boats had no way to
send a warning. The "hardest blow" got harder still, picking up
steam as it swept into the Choptank. Nearly a dozen boats out
of Cambridge, Md. were working various Choptank oyster bars

that day—Benoni Bar, Howell Point, Chloris, and Castle Haven among them.

These boats, too, were on their way home. If the storm had come through an hour later they would have been tied up, safe and sound. The conditions were different on the Choptank, with a fog so thick that no one saw the sky turn black off on the horizon the way those Bay boats had. When the storm hit, one witness said, it was as if "a curtain dropped over the sun."

The writer Christopher White pored through old newspaper articles and interviewed survivors to piece together what happened next. His dramatic account of the storm appears in the book *Skipjack: The Story of America's Last Sailing Oystermen.* Here is White:

When it was 100 yards away, it looked like black smoke over the water. No whitecaps. The wind was faster than the waves.

Here is Willie Parks, crewman on the *Joy Parks*:

That storm bore down on us like a rushing freight train.

Here is Will Jones of the *J.T. Leonard*:

Skunk. That's what we call 'em. A squall that sneaks up on you.

The storm blew the topsail off of the *Leonard*. The crew couldn't get the mainsail down. The storm had control of the boat. Jones:

We couldn't do a thing but hang on and hope. Couldn't get the dredges in. They were jumping up and down behind us like porpoises.

139

Another boat, the *Agnes*, never had a chance, capsizing near Howell Point. Five men died. The *Annie Lee* capsized, too. Five men went overboard. Four died. More on the survivor in a moment. The crew of the bugeye *Nora Lawson* got lucky—when she capsized, the men aboard found themselves in shallow water. Everyone survived.

He Had Just 'One Chance to Throw a Line'
The story of how George Wheatley survived is hard to believe. The lone survivor from the *Annie Lee*, he was working on the motor in the yawl trailing that boat when the storm hit. As he would recall:

The Annie Lee went down quick. And the yawl went down with her. There is a skiff at the back of the yawl and I got in it.

The skiff soon capsized. Wheatley and his four shipmates were all wearing hip waders, which filled with water and dragged them toward the bottom. All five managed to get those waders off. They bobbed back up to the surface. Soon everyone was holding onto that little overturned skiff. Somebody managed to grab hold of an anchor line and steady that little boat, then lost hold of the line.

The men knew they wouldn't survive in the water for long. This was February. Hypothermia would kill them in short order. One by one they tried to get out of the icy water by climbing atop that skiff, but every climb ended in that skiff flipping over. Four men went under.

Only Wheatley remained. Somehow, at the tender age of 19, he had seen the situation more clearly than his more experienced shipmates. Whenever one of them tried to climb atop that

140

skiff, he opted to let go of the skiff. Only after each flip would he dog paddle back up to it and grab hold again.

The fog, the storm, the frantic work of self-preservation: How in God's name did Capt. Bill Hubbard of the *Geneva May* spot Wheatley out there? Hubbard didn't have complete control of his boat—that wind was still blowing. But he couldn't just abandon a fellow waterman out there without trying. Writer Christopher White:

The skipjack was bearing down on Wheatley at full speed with the wind behind her. She was flying.

Hubbard had one chance to throw a line as he zipped by, and Wheatley had one chance to catch it. They got it done. But catching the line meant nothing if Wheatley couldn't hold on once that line from the flying skipjack pulled taut. He put the knotted end in his teeth. He looped the rope around his arms. He didn't have time to do anything else. Christopher White:

As the line became taut he held the line with both fists on either side of his mouth. This man was not letting go. The boat rushed by. The abrupt yank on the line, as it took hold, nearly broke his neck ... Wheatley planed atop the river like a body surfer.

Aboard the *Geneva May*, crew members spliced their end of Wheatley's lifeline onto the dredge cable and started winding the surfer in. White again:

With a smack, his body slammed into the side of the boat, and the crew reeled him up ... like a load of oysters.

Wheatley was shivering violently when he came aboard. His skin was purple. He passed out almost immediately. His rescuers covered him in blankets.

'I Didn't Think a Single Boat Would Come Back'

The storm that ravaged the Choptank that day marched across the Delmarva Peninsula but killed no one else. It blew out a huge window in the lobby of the Hotel Sussex in Seaford, Del. It tore the roof off a chicken hatchery in nearby Middleford. Tree limbs and other debris littered roadways all over southern Delaware. That day's weather was insane not just around the Chesapeake, but across half the country. Floods killed at least five people in the Ohio Valley. Three tornadoes touched down in South Carolina. Offshore winds drove ships aground off New England. Blizzards shut down highways in Indiana, Missouri, and elsewhere.

Waterman Sangston Todd spoke for all of the oystermen who returned home:

I never expected to set foot [on land] again.

Ivy McNamara:

All of us are lucky to be here. I didn't think a single boat would come back.

Countless boats joined in the search for the dead in the days that followed. Seven bodies turned up. Two were never found. Here are the names of the five men from the *Agnes* who lost their lives: Capt. William Bradford, Aaron Ennals, Rodney Jones, Robert Elliott, and Herbert Robinson. At age 77 Bradford was probably the oldest captain working in the Chesapeake region at that point. The

142

four men who lost their lives from the *Annie Lee*: Capt. Theodore Wooden, Emerson Wingate, Clem Roberts, and Samuel Brown.

As for the miracle man, George Wheatley, he made a full recovery, then returned to oystering the next season. Here is what he told White many years later:

I was only nineteen then. I thought I was invincible. Nothing bad could happen to me. Then I nearly died. By all accounts I should've died. But I didn't give up the fight. I was a waterman all my life. It's what I am. I figured if I capsized again I'd fight all the harder. This life is worth fighting for.

In addition to putting in many more years on the water, Wheatley would work jobs as an oyster broker and as a custodian at a public school. He passed away in 2009 at the age of 88.

19 FORGIVENESS
EVEN FREDERICK DOUGLASS HAS SOMETHING TO APOLOGIZE FOR

Let's pretend we're walking in the shoes of Frederick Douglass. We're talking here about a man who left gargantuan footprints on American history, so that metaphorical footwear is gonna to be way too big. But play along and we'll wobble our way toward an extraordinary gesture of apology that unfolded on the Delmarva Peninsula in the aftermath of the Civil War.

Perhaps you've seen photos of Douglass in his elder-statesman years. The penetrating eyes, that tailored suit, the snow-white hair, an impeccably trimmed beard. That's likely how he looked in June of 1877 when stepping off a steamboat in St. Michaels, Md. at Navy Point, a spot that's part of the Chesapeake Bay Maritime Museum today. He was returning at sixtyish years old to his home turf of Maryland's Eastern Shore, where he'd been born into slavery.

Snapshot of a Great Man
Many folks are familiar with the arc of Douglass's life, while oth-

ers might need a quick refresher. Let's sum up the complex story of an American hero in three quick bullet points.

• Fred Bailey spent his earliest years in a little cabin on a remote stretch of Tuckahoe Creek in Talbot County, Md. He never knew who his father was. Perhaps it was the white man who owned his mother. He barely knew that mother—she always seemed to be toiling on faraway farms. When his original owner died Fred was inherited by a man named Thomas Auld.

• Bleak circumstances be damned: Fred developed a passion for self-improvement and education at an absurdly early age. Consider how he learned to read. He never attended school, but he landed at one point in the home of a white woman who taught him some rudimentary facts about the alphabet. That woman's husband put a stop to those lessons right quick, but Fred was off and running. He taught himself the rest, piecing the sounds and symbols that woman had showed him into words and sentences. By his teen years he was taking deep dives into the works of famed orators from Roman times.

• Fred escaped slavery at 20. He rechristened himself as Frederick Douglass and made his way to upstate New York. There he blazed a trail that would turn him into one of the most famous and honored men of his time. Those hard-won, self-taught skills as orator and writer became powerful weapons in the abolitionist cause. He became a great champion of human freedom.

A Secret Agenda in St. Michaels
Back to St. Michaels in 1877. Douglass spent a good amount of time in those days on the lecture circuit. Giving a talk was the

public reason for his visit. But the most interesting thing that happened on this visit was more of a private affair—a face-to-face meeting with Thomas Auld.

A *Baltimore Sun* scribe who was tagging along on the St. Michaels trip quoted Douglass:

I came, first of all, to see my old master, from whom I have been separated for 41 years.

Other accounts, including one Douglass himself wrote four years later, say it was Auld who invited Douglass to stop by. But that doesn't really matter. More from Douglass, according to that *Baltimore Sun* scribe:

[I want] to shake his hand, to look into his kind old face.

I first came across this quote when I was deep into researching Douglass's life. My face twisted in disbelief at that "kind old face" business, then twisted some more when it became apparent that Douglass planned to offer his former owner some sort of an apology. My research had left me with a different idea about what Douglass should do upon seeing Auld.

Maybe punch him in the nose?

Love and Hate in Slavery Times
Thomas Auld "owned" Fred Bailey for a dozen years, starting when Fred was 8. Historians have spilled gallons of ink debating the nature of their relationship. Some see it as a straightforward affair: Douglass hated his onetime owner, and for good reason.

Others see great complexity. There was no father in young Fred's life. His mother (through no fault of her own) was missing in action. He was separated from a beloved grandmother early on as well. Did Auld, by default, become the paternalish figure in Fred's formative years? Was there a dysfunctional family dynamic lingering in Fred's heart even many decades later, a combustible mix of evil owner on one hand and father figure on the other?

If you look hard enough, you can find moments when Auld treated Fred in ways that can be seen as kindly, as least when judged by the standards of slavery times. Twice, Auld sent young Fred to live and toil in the Baltimore home of his brother, Hugh Auld. Fred preferred big city life. Though still enslaved he had a degree of autonomy in Baltimore that opened windows of self-governed time. It was in those windows that he pursued his passion for self-education. On another occasion, after a failed escape attempt, Auld backed off from a threat to sell Fred off and ship him to the Deep South.

But Auld also treated Fred with horrifying cruelty. The worst of those offenses unfolded in Fred's teenage years. He had been pulled out of Baltimore and plopped back at Auld's home in St. Michaels. Word got out among local blacks that this newly arrived big city boy could read. Fred agreed to try and teach that skill to local blacks.

It didn't go well. Angry white men armed with sticks and clubs busted up the first class. Auld was furious with Fred. Auld's white neighbors demanded that he punish the "uppity" slave who had dared try and teach "their" blacks to read.

Auld chose a punishment that was beyond the pale. He sent Fred to the farm of Stephen Covey, a man who specialized in "breaking" rebellious slaves. On Covey's farm Fred endured the worst of slavery, an endless barrage of psychological torture mixed with physical beatings. Slowly but surely, this bright, highly motivated young man sank into a depressed state, "broken in body, soul, and spirit."

Bloodied, and Begging for Mercy

Fred was working one of Covey's farm fields on a steamy August afternoon when he collapsed, presumably from heat stroke. The slave breaker responded not with medical help or even so much as a glass of water, but by beating the prone teenager mercilessly.

Fred couldn't take any more. He fled the Covey farm—not running away from slavery, just running away from that beating. He soon showed up five or six miles away, back in St. Michaels, at the doorstep of his owner. He begged Thomas Auld to take him back in, to save him from Covey.

I presented an appearance of wretchedness and woe. From the crown of my head to the sole of my feet there were marks of blood. My hair was all clotted with dust and blood, and the back of my shirt was literally stiff with the same.

Briefly, hope: Auld looked dismayed at Fred's bloody appearance. But that look passed quickly, replaced by an expression "cold and hard as iron." Auld ordered Fred to march right back to the slave breaker's farm.

A Weapon in the War on Slavery

Fast forward a few decades, to the point where Douglass had escaped bondage and become a leader in the antislavery movement. He went after Thomas Auld with avengeance, sharing many tales of mistreatment, including that one about the slave breaker. The speeches Douglass delivered in this window often reached an emotional crescendo when he turned his back to the audience and pulled down his shirt, revealing scars from whippings. Auld put some of those scars there.

One polemic Douglass wrote was especially effective. In "A Letter to My Old Master," Douglass made a public promise to Thomas Auld.

I intend to make use of you as a weapon with which to assail the system of slavery ... as a means of bringing this guilty nation, with yourself, to repent.

What in the world would leave Douglass feeling in his elder statesman years like he should apologize to such a man?

The Big Picture of 1877
By the time Douglass arrived in St. Michaels in 1877, he had heard that Thomas Auld was in a sickly, bedridden state. He thought Auld was on his deathbed, though the man would cling to life for two and a half more years.

The Civil War was a dozen years in the past, but the dream of reconciliation between the races was fraying. Earlier that year President Rutherford B. Hayes had pulled the plug on the faltering Reconstruction programs. Black folks looked to be back on the downswing, sinking into a second-class brand of citizenship that might not be slavery, but was far from the full freedom they'd been promised.

Douglass still ranked as a big celebrity in those postwar years. He had stints in a then-prominent post as U.S. marshal and as ambassador to Haiti. On speaking tours, he was always urging blacks to embrace up-by-the-bootstraps self-improvement and telling whites they should welcome black progress as key to a brighter American future.

That's the kind of talk he gave to a mixed-race crowd in

St. Michaels. Afterward, Douglass got word from a messenger. Given those conflicting reports about who initiated this meeting, that message was either an unprompted invitation from Auld or a positive reply to Douglass's request for a meeting.

Word spread through the crowd. Douglass biographer David Blight:

A gawking entourage followed him from Navy Point to the corner of Cherry Street and Locust Lane.

Douglass led that rabble up to a building that serves today as the Dodson House bed and breakfast. Back then it belonged to Louisa Bruff, a daughter of Thomas Auld. Accompanied by a small entourage of reporters and friends, Douglass soon arrived in the bedridden man's room.

Let's pause here to make sure and say one big picture thing: There is no question in the big sweep of history that Douglass was on the noble and just side of the fight against slavery.

There were some niggling questions, however, that arose over a couple of the details Douglass had used while waging that public-relations war against his former owner. The key for-instance: Douglass accused Auld of abandoning Douglass's beloved grandmother in her old age, once she was no longer physically able to do the work of a slave.

My grandmother was now very old, her frame already wracked with the pains of old age, and complete helplessness fast stealing over her once active limbs. They took her to the woods and built her a little hut and then made her welcome to the privilege of supporting herself there in perfect loneliness; thus virtually turning her out to die.

This qualified as a serious offense back then. I know it sounds like an oxymoron, but there really were some generally accepted moral standards among slave owners. One such rule obliged them to provide basic necessities of life to such elderly slaves.

Auld claimed this story about the grandmother was false. He said that she was legally in the control of other owners at the time she was "turned out" and that the moment he found out what had happened to her, he set about fixing things so she wouldn't have to worry about food and shelter.

The Meeting Unfolds
This business about the grandmother is a topic Douglass wanted to address with Auld. The two exchanged simple but formal greetings.

Captain Auld! (He used to be a ship captain.)

Marshal Douglass!

Douglass had heard that Auld was sickly, but the sight of his condition still came as a shock. Was this frail creature really the same man who'd been such an all-powerful figure in his younger years?

The sight of him, the changes which time had wrought in him, his tremulous hands constantly in motion, and all the circumstances of his condition affected me deeply, and for a time choked my voice and made me speechless. We both, however, got the better of our feelings, and conversed freely about the past.

Then came the apology. Douglass "grasped the palsied hand of Captain Auld."

*I told him that I had made a mistake in my narrative [by] ...
attributing to him ungrateful and cruel treatment of my grandmother.*

A media brouhaha erupted over this and a couple of other turns in
the conversation. At one point Douglass tried to break the formal-
ity of the session by telling Auld to address him as "Frederick."
But that gesture showed up in newspapers as the much more
subservient sounding, "Call me Fred."

   Pro-slavery folks in the South had a field day. A southern
newspaper published a cartoon that got picked up by other publications in the former Confederate states, showing the "great"
Frederick Douglass on his knees before his former master. The
exchange also gave ammunition to Douglass's critics on the anti-
slavery Party of Lincoln side of the aisle. Some of them thought
the once-great man had gone soft in his older years. The *New
York Times* got into the act:

*It would appear that Mr. Fred. Douglass's role as a leader of his
race is about played out.*

In the set-the-record-straight piece Douglass wrote in 1881 he
dismissed this media hubbub as "the work of heartless triflers."
He made clear that he had apologized to Auld not in submissive
fashion, but as one free man to another. Why? I don't think that
answer is complicated. He'd gotten some of those grandmother
facts wrong. And when a writer makes such mistakes—even
about a man who's earned a strong measure of hatred—he or she
should own up to it.

   Later in the meeting Douglas asked Auld how he felt those

many years ago, when young Fred Bailey had run away for good and made it to freedom in the north. That led to this famously heartfelt-sounding exchange.

Auld: *I always knew you were too smart to be a slave and had I been in your place. I should have done as you did.*

Douglass: *I am glad to hear you say this. I did not run away from you, but from slavery. It was not that I loved Caesar less, but Rome more.*

Twenty Minutes Full of Mystery
By Douglass's account this meeting lasted all of 20 minutes. Historians have been going back and forth for many decades now, churning out theories about the deep meaning of this brief conversation. Let's briefly run through three of those theories.

First. The meeting marked an end-of-life moment of reconciliation between two men embroiled in a long, complicated, dysfunctional emotional cauldron of a relationship between an owner and slave who also regarded each other as father figure and stand-in son. Call this the Dickson Preston theory.

The David Blight theory is that Douglass's apology wasn't really tied up with all this love/hate business. Rather it came from a yearning inside of Douglass's own heart. He had reached a stage that had him grappling with the meaning of his life's work and perhaps struggling with some self-doubts. Had he really lived a life that matched all his noble words?

In much of the Christian tradition—in which Douglass had learned to think and write—the forgiver often forgives for his own sake, not to excuse the oppressor. He forgives to strengthen his own heart, to work through grief, pain, loss, and hatred. ... [It was] Douglass [who] needed this meeting most.

Our third theorizer, Robert Levine, doesn't think Douglass brought any real emotional baggage into the meeting. He thinks Douglass met Auld for reasons that were strictly strategic—he wanted to put on a show for the press and the public. Part of that show was a demonstration of power. This wasn't a meeting between two equals—Douglass was the famous guy here, deigning to meet a sickly little nobody who had once owned him. Which one of the two had an entourage?

Remember how Reconstruction efforts were faltering? By apologizing to Auld, Levine says, Douglass was looking to keep hope alive, to show the nation and its leaders in vivid and dramatic fashion that reconciliation between the races really was possible. This conversation was just another workmanlike moment for Douglass. He was trying, as he did most every day, to do what needed doing to advance the cause of human freedom.

Of the Forest and the Trees
This debate was interesting stuff. It held my attention while I was down in that rabbit hole. But I came back out with a shrug of indifference over the question of which emotions were swirling around that room in St. Michaels in 1877.

Instead, I was struck, as I had been time and again in my research, by the image of Douglass as inspiring role model. I ended up seeing this deathbed exchange as a three-in-one instructional manual for thinking about what to do in our modern lives with messy, complex relationships.

• If what Douglass did was apologize sincerely for a mistake and reach out a hand of friendship to a sickly old man with whom he'd had a tortured love/hate relationship, well, God bless him for putting his enmity aside.

• If what Douglass did was apologize not so much to the dying man, but in a sincere effort to cleanse his troubled soul and prove he could live up to his own noble ideals, well, God bless him for being worthy of God's grace.

• If what Douglass did was stage a fake apology in a feigned public relations show of human sympathy with a hated enemy, well, God bless him for putting the cause of human freedom above his repulsion at saying "I'm sorry" to an evil old SOB.

Whichever theory you like, Douglass displayed simple human decency. Those metaphorical shoes of his were even bigger than I had imagined.

20 RESILIENCE
THE GIMPY GRAND MARSHAL
OF FREEDOM

Had the world turned upside down? So it must have looked
to many white folks in Key West, Fla. on Jan. 29, 1863. Two
hundred and fifty black men embarked on a celebratory march
through the streets that Thursday. Hundreds of happy women and
children traipsed alongside.

A few angry white folks threw stones, but the killjoys
couldn't dampen the mood—the black community was celebrating the Emancipation Proclamation, the end of slavery. Marchers
dressed in their Sunday best, none more so than the seventy-
something-year-old community patriarch leading the way—black
suit, bright rose corsage, and a ceremonial saber to complete the
ensemble.

*He is large-headed, large-souled, big of stature, full of vigor and
brawn, and the most perfect gentleman in Key West.*

The patriarch walked with a limp, but his slow pace didn't bother
anyone. Everyone in the parade knew the story behind that old
injury, and they regarded his faltering gait as something to be cel-

ebrated, a powerful, perfect symbol for what so many black folks had endured—and now, overcome—in slavery times.

This chapter will tell the story behind that limp, but first, a public service announcement: Self-mutilation is never a good idea. If you're tempted, reach for help.

Next, a trite truism: There's an exception to every rule.

The exception in this case is that gimpy old man. His name was Sandy Cornish.

Eastern Shore Beginnings

Cornish was born into slavery on Maryland's Eastern Shore in 1793, the "property" of a man named William Eccleston. A family of that name lived in North Dorchester County in this window—old land records have William Eccleston taking ownership in the 1770s of 380 acres in the vicinity of the present-day towns of Hurlock and East New Market.

Cornish said later in life that he never worked the fields as a young man. He toiled more as some sort of a manservant. When William died, a son of his assumed ownership of Cornish. Things took an unusual turn. The records and oral history on this are thin, so there's a little guesswork involved on my part. It looks like that son didn't want or need another laborer around. But neither did he want to grant Cornish his freedom. So that new owner told Cornish to go off wherever he liked, get a job, and take care of himself.

But Cornish would need to pay for this "privilege," to the tune of $83 a year.

Cornish is in his mid-40s at this point. He's married to a free black woman named Lillah. By all accounts he cut quite the imposing figure in his prime. Folks who knew him a little later in life gushed over "the physique of a prize fighter," a "body round as a barrel," and muscles like on a "racehorse's leg."

Once Sandy got that quasi-brand of freedom for an annual fee, he and Lillah made a weird-seeming decision. They moved to the Deep South, relocating to the Florida panhandle town of Port Leon in late 1839 or early 1840. The town doesn't exist anymore, save for a smattering of ghost-town remnants in the modern-day St. Marks National Wildlife Refuge, below Tallahassee.

But Port Leon was a bustling place then, filled with laborers constructing a new railroad line. Cornish got a job on that line that paid him $600 a year. He and Lillah didn't live high on the hog, however. It took them nine long years to save the princely sum of $3,200.

With that, Sandy Cornish bought his own freedom.

Back on the Brink of Slavery

Alas, the hopes he and Lillah had for a new life free from bondage went up in smoke, quite literally. A fire tore through Port Leon, leveling homes and government buildings full of civic records. Sandy and Lillah kept most all of their money in cash. That was gone. Worse: The paperwork that proved Cornish was a free man burned up, too.

Port Leon was a Wild West sort of place. Those rough and tumble railroad workers were fond of gambling, drinking, carousing, and, sometimes, criminal activity. Word got out about Cornish's burned-up paperwork. He was kidnapped by a gang of white guys who planned to take him to New Orleans, sell him as a slave, and pocket the cash.

Somehow, Cornish slipped out of the ropes that bound him. A round of fisticuffs followed. Cornish escaped the gang, making a run for it. But he didn't try to find a hiding place. Nor did he run to the cops—there wasn't much in the way of justice available to black men in the South in those days.

Instead, he went back home to Lillah. Perhaps Cornish had already decided on his own what to do. Or perhaps he ran his predicament by his wife and together he and Lillah concocted a plan that seems ... well ... it's pure insanity.

First step, gather supplies. That meant needles, thread, plaster, a knife, an axe, and a mirror.

The couple marched together toward the center of town, pushing that weird mix of supplies in a wheelbarrow. The whole way, Cornish screamed like a banshee at the top of his lungs. He hollered the same thing over and over, ordering everyone within earshot to come out and watch what he was about to do.

A crowd gathered. Black, white, men, women. Then, with the whole town watching, Cornish set about making himself worthless on the slave market. If Hollywood made a movie about Cornish's life—perhaps they should!—this is a scene you wouldn't be able to watch. You'd cover your eyes in horror. Consider yourself warned about the next few paragraphs.

Cornish pulled out the knife and sliced up one of his ankles. Then he plunged the knife into his hip joint, carving a giant gash. He picked up the axe next and chopped at the fingers of his left hand. One finger fell clean off. Journalist Whitelaw Reid's description of this scene is based on an interview with Cornish himself.

Finally, brandishing the bloody knife, Sandy shouted to the crowd that if they persisted in their effort to sell a free man into slavery after he had once bought himself out of it, his right arm was yet strong, and he had one blow reserved [for any man who tried to put him on the auction block].

159

Reid uses dialect in quoting what Cornish said to the crowd:

I [told everyone] I would cut open my belly and put de entrals before 'em. But dat I wouldn't go to New Orleans [and become] a slave agin, for I was free.

The white people in the crowd walked away, presumably muttering about the insanity of it all. Many black folks stuck around, however. They watched as Sandy and Lillah got to work on part two of the plan.

Lillah threaded a needle. She handed it to her husband. Then she picked up that mirror and positioned it just so, near the ankle that Cornish had sliced. Peering into that mirror, Cornish commenced stitching himself up with needle and thread. Then he spread plaster over the wound. Next, the hip. Then, the fingers. While preparing to sew back that one finger he'd cut clean off, he put the digit in his mouth, like "a cigar."

Those black folks pitched in once the sewing and plastering was done. They lifted Cornish up and laid him in that wheelbarrow. Neighbors drove him back home.

Sandy Cornish didn't get out of bed for six months. But he'd done a decent job with that needle and thread. First, he tried hobbling on crutches. After a year he could limp around without them. He regained the use of his fingers, too.

And he got back to living as a free man.

The Patriarch of Key West
Historians haven't come across any words directly from Sandy or Lillah saying why they moved to Key West in about 1850, but it's a destination that makes sense for their situation. Founded in the 1820s, the town prospered from the get-go. Its population had

grown to nearly 3,000 by the time the Cornishes arrived, including 125 or so free blacks. The place was a magnet for adventurers and entrepreneurs. It ranked in those years as the richest town in the country when measured on a per-capita basis.

Sandy's name is mostly missing from public records, but Lillah's name pops up. She's listed as the buyer of two lots on what was then called Division Street—it's called Truman Avenue today, the main drag—at Simonton Street. The Cornishes had nearly 20 acres of farmland east of there.

They grew 4,000 pounds of produce annually—grapes, guavas, oranges, coconuts, tamarind, and more. Sandy and Lillah even grew bushes full of what one writer describes as "West African cayenne pepper berries." The couple ran the place like an 1850s version of one of our modern-day farmer's markets, serving up plates of food for 50 cents and even offering entertainment in a little "piazza." It seems the folks in Key West were fond of fortune tellers.

When the Civil War erupted, Key West remained insulated from the worst abuses of Confederate soldiers, slaveholders, and their supporters. The federal government had one fort in town and another just offshore—the place was in Union hands throughout the conflict.

Soldiers stationed at those forts were reportedly some of Sandy and Lillah's best customers. He was quite the popular figure with the men in blue—in 1862, a group of soldiers from Pennsylvania celebrating New Year's Eve "roused" Cornish in the middle of the night just to give him a raucous "salute."

Cornish became one of the richest men in the richest town in America. He was quite famous, too—the legend of what he'd done in Port Leon spread far and wide during his Key West years.

Since the war, his remarkable history has attracted many visitors ... and brought him many attentions that might readily have turned the head of a less judicious person. but Sandie pursues his quiet way, modest as ever, and still industrious and money-making.

That journalist I mentioned, Whitelaw Reid, met Cornish while reporting on a postwar fact-finding tour of the South by U.S. Supreme Court Justice Salmon Chase and other federal officials. After arriving in Key West, those officials kept hearing that the "main feature" of their upcoming "ride around the island" would be "a visit to Old Sandie's farm."

Fresh produce was hard to come by in Key West before the Cornishes came to town. Sandy and Lillah were apparently the first to figure out how to get fruits and vegetables to grow abundantly in salty, rocky soil.

Sandy greeted those VIPs "in a faultless suit of broadcloth, with a well-brushed silk hat." His guests soon learned that they, like everyone else in town, should call Lillah "auntie." Cornish was 73 years old as this point, but Reid saw a man who qualified as an ageless wonder.

[He is] the strongest man on the island, the richest of the negroes, the best farmer here, and with a history as romantic as that of any Indian whom song and story have combined to make famous.

The legend of Sandy Cornish lives on. A church congregation he helped found worships in Key West as Cornish Memorial AME Zion. A sculpture of Cornish stands alongside other civic heroes in the Key West Historic Memorial Sculpture Garden. Every February, Florida newspapers and schoolteachers tell his story.

Cornish most likely died in 1869. I wonder if Lillah pinned a corsage to the suit he was buried in, just as she had six years before when Sandy stepped into a starring role he so richly deserved—as the gimpy grand marshal of a civic parade that marked a new birth of freedom.

21 NEIGHBORS
Across the Great Divide with a Talbot County Socialite

Imagine it's 1941. You're living among the highest of high-society cliques on the Eastern Shore of Maryland. The Talbot County landscape of Miles River Neck you call home is dotted with old plantations and peopled with the descendants of rich slaveholding families. The story at hand here is partly about race relations, so remember, too, that 1941 was segregation times.

You go out to the mailbox. Among the usual bills is an oversized envelope, probably an invitation. Perhaps you roll your eyes: "Ugh, not another socialite party!" Then you open it.

A Sacred Outing
At the home of Mrs. Ruth Starr Rose on the Miles River
Sunday, June 22
Sponsored by Deshields Church, Copperville
The JUNIOR-SENIOR SONGSTERS, a group of 50 voices of Waugh Church Cambridge, Md. will render the musical selections.

Well, now! Both churches mentioned are chock full of history, but not in a way that fits our modern-day preconceptions of segregation times. Deshields and Waugh are black churches. The invitation lists a program of songs, all African-American spirituals—"I Am Leaning on the Lord," "Home in Dat Rock," and "Couldn't Hear Nobody Pray," among others. At the bottom is a footnote:

It is the special request of Mrs. Rose that both races attend this outing.

Yes, this is a story about a white socialite who invited black people over to her ritzy estate. But Ruth Starr Rose didn't just take that small step across the color barrier. She was more like a gold-medal-winning Olympian hurdler of race relations, bounding over barrier after barrier in the race of her life.

She was a painter as well as a socialite. Her favorite subject was her working-class black neighbors. James Porter of Howard University, who pretty much invented the field of African American art history, had this to say in 1956 about the work Rose created:

Ruth Starr Rose's visual interpretation of Negro Spirituals is the most comprehensive and probably the most sympathetic work yet to appear in the United States. Although Negro Spirituals have been interpreted by numerous artists in many different media ... no single artist has approached the extensive treatment accorded by this artist to this theme.

That Socialite Pedigree
We all make the blunder now and again of ignoring that saying

about how first appearances can be deceiving. We hear a snippet about this stranger's life. We see the way that stranger dresses. We notice a bumper sticker on some other stranger's car. Off we go: "That's my kind of person!" Or: "What a jerk!"

It works the same way in history. Ruth Starr Rose had a "Lifestyles of the Rich and Famous" pedigree of the sort that might lead to first-impression insults. Take your pick: "Socialite," "trust-fund baby," "spoiled rich girl," "child of privilege." Dig deeper, however, and you'll see that we could all use her names as a three-syllable mantra to guard against judging folks before we know them.

Let's review her "Lifestyles of the Rich and Famous" re-sume. First, family tree. On her mother's side was a signer of the Declaration of Independence. On the other side was a founder of what would become Harvard University. Her paternal grandfather was a big politico in the early days of Wisconsin. Her father made a fortune in timbering and other ventures.

Ruth entered the world in 1887, silver spoon set in mouth. The daughter of Ida May and William Rose got diplomas from the exclusive National Cathedral School in Washington, DC and the even more exclusive Vassar College in upstate New York.

She landed on the Eastern Shore as a teenager. In 1906 her Wisconsinite parents bought the Hope House plantation on Miles River Neck. In the 1700s that property had been owned by famously wealthy members of the Lloyd and Tilghman fami-lies. The place was a wreck by the time the Roses arrived. A tree was growing through the roof, leaving big chunks of the interior exposed to the elements. Ruth's mother, Ida May, broke into tears upon seeing the place. She accused her husband of buying "a view, a stair rail, and a cemetery—that's all!"

The Roses dropped a chunk of their fortune into a meticulous renovation and then got about the business of high-society living. William had Easton boatbuilder George W. Jackson make him a 79-foot power yacht, *Esperanza*. Ruth loved sailboats and became quite accomplished at racing her log canoe, *Belle M. Crane*.

One last "Lifestyles" tidbit. When Ruth married the wealthy New York City businessman William Rose in June 1914, she wore what one newspaper story described as a "dress of Callot satin." At the time, Callot Soeurs of Paris was the pinnacle of the fashion world. Pearls, sapphires, and a diamond necklace accented that gown.

The 300 guests at her nuptials found Hope House "surpassing in beauty and elaborateness," awash in thousands of floral blooms. Easter lilies were the theme in one room, pink roses in another. Guests strolled under an arched arbor to reach an expansive lawn, site of the evening's entertainment.

After nightfall the four hundred Japanese lanterns lighting the lawn, the music of the Philadelphia Orchestra ... and the costumes of the ladies all made for an [atmosphere] of exceptional splendor and appeal.

The young couple settled into their ritzy life, splitting time between homes on Miles River Neck and in the New York City area. They would eventually adopt two children. They never had to worry much about money.

The Threads that Lead to Copperville
A couple other threads in Ruth's background are worth unraveling here. First up, art. Ida May Rose studied music in Europe with a famous composer, Clara Schumann. She also excelled

at landscape design. She wrote a two-volume history of Caribbean gardens. After restoring Hope House Ida May set about turning the grounds there into one of Maryland's finest gardens. One newspaper story after another in the decades that followed sang awestruck praises of her work on that front. Ruth's brother, Nathan Comfort Starr became a college professor specializing in Medieval literature. Nathan married the photographer and art historian Nina Howell Starr.

Painting was Ruth's artsy passion. She studied it at Vassar and later signed on with the Art Students League of New York, a collective chock full of notable artists. Generally speaking, the League attracted members who rejected the abstract and avant-garde trends of the time in favor of an "American Scene" style focused on working-class subjects and scenes of everyday living. Ruth moved in impressive creative circles, counting singer Paul Robeson and film director Orson Welles among her friends.

The other thread touches on race relations. Rose's paternal grandfather, a prominent businessman in Wisconsin, came to the defense of a guy who had helped an escaped slave in 1860, violating one of the Fugitive Slave acts. That episode led to a big civic meeting, chaired by the grandfather, that ended in a call to form a "League of Freedom"—basically, an armed local militia determined to fight off anyone who tried to capture runaway slaves.

The 20th century Roses brought a measure of that commitment to racial reconciliation to Hope House. In addition to those sprawling old plantations, the Miles River Neck landscape has a trio of tiny African American communities—Tunis Mills, Unionville, and Copperville. These enclaves sprung up after the Civil War, peopled by both newly freed slaves and laborers who'd been legally "free" in slavery times, but often oppressed nonetheless. Union army Colored Troop veterans were in the mix, too.

Before it was incorporated Copperville had an evocative nickname—the "Village of Liberty." Frederick Douglass spent some time in bondage on Miles River Neck. His family roots on his mother's side are here, and some descendants of his family still live in the area today. It's these communities—especially Copperville—that became the focus of Ruth Starr Rose's artistic energies.

'They Have Always Given Me as Much as I Have Given Them'

There doesn't seem to have been a magic moment when Ruth Starr Rose shifted into her Olympian hurdler mode. Ruth's mother took her teenage daughter to services at the black Deshields church in Copperville during their first year of living in Talbot County. Like other nearby plantations Hope House employed African American labor for all kinds of tasks—gardening, cooking, housekeeping, etc. Ruth spoke several times over the years about how the way those boss/worker relationships blossomed into true friendships.

Barbara Paca, a curator who has worked tirelessly in recent years to bring Ruth Starr Rose and her work back into prominence, makes an important observation in her book, *There Is a City Called Heaven*. Ruth didn't play the role of heroic rich-girl "missionary" helper. She dove much more deeply than that into the communal, intellectual, and spiritual world of her neighbors:

I admire the great dignity of the Negroes. I like their old people and their children ... [T]hey have always given me as much as I have given them.

We cannot help the colored people by stooping down, we have to

169

stand on the same level and together find the light.

Ruth worshipped regularly at Deshields over the course of several decades. She taught Sunday school classes there. The picnic she threw in 1941 wasn't a one-off event. She threw similar parties most every year, advertising the affairs in local papers and charging admission to benefit Deshields church.

At the Water's Edge

We're lucky here in the 21st century because it's pretty easy to get up close and personal with the art of Ruth Starr Rose. The best option is to visit the Water's Edge Museum in Oxford, Md. Second best is wandering the website of that museum.

Online and in person the facility is mostly devoted to displaying Rose's work and telling her story and the stories of her black neighbors. I'm not an art critic, so I don't have the vocabulary to wax eloquent about brush strokes and visual styles. What I can say is that Water's Edge left me with the feeling that I'd traveled back a century and enjoyed a priceless experience, getting to meet and greet the people of old Copperville.

One intriguing character after another awaits—a young duck hunter, a guitarist, a little boy all gussied up for church. The most famous of Rose's portraits depicts Anna May Moaney, a domestic servant presented as the personification of strength, dignity, and style. Barbara Paca regards that portrait as a kind of "black Mona Lisa."

There are no caricatures in sight. Rose imbued her subjects with a depth of emotion and personality that was rarely accorded to black subjects in her day, not to mention in the centuries before that. Other works at Water's Edge bring back to life hundred-year-old scenes of daily doings in and around Copperville—a circus in town, crabpickers at work, a sailmaker toiling away at his craft.

The other major strand in Rose's work is the one that so impressed that art historian, James Porter—her artistic renditions of African-American spirituals.

These songs that I heard every day welled from the hearts of a people, sung with religious fervor that made me feel humble.

"Glory Train" has an angel-powered, white-smoke-belching locomotive swirling toward heaven with an angelic escort in the sky over Deshields Church. Passengers are waving at the people left on the church grounds. Rose got the notion for this treatment while seeing the local Moaney Quartet perform "This Train is Bound for Glory." They didn't just sing the hymn—they performed it in theatrical fashion, stomping around the church, shouting and rumbling and singing in ways that had the whole congregation striving to mimic the sound of a train engine starting up for a journey to the hereafter. The Moaney Quartet had a way, Rose said, of making "the shivers run down your back as you sit in the stiff-backed pew."

In 1940 the congregation at Deshields asked Rose to create a mural for display behind the pulpit. Rose wondered later in life if perhaps she was the first white artist ever invited to create a work for a black church. The subject she chose was "Pharaoh's Army Got Drownd'd," the parting of the Red Sea. That sea really is red, with a long line of the black faithful making their way along a magical passage in the water while bathed in divine light and under the watchful guidance of a horn-blowing angel. The writer of a profile of Rose that appeared in the *Christian Science Monitor* in 1953 reported:

All agreed that it was entirely permissible for the artist to put a steamboat on the Red Sea.

'One of the Wonders of the New World'

How did Ruth Starr Rose view her mission in life, and in art? I think the best way to communicate that is to get out of the way and let the woman herself talk. Here are a few quotes from various books and articles:

These allegorical interpretations attempt, through design, color, and integration of life elements, to bring about unity between the races, by means of paint.

You can't dramatize the feelings of a people that have come out of great suffering unless you share their ideals. I believe it was religion that brought the Negroes out of suffering.

One night at the Copperville church, the handsome brown leader of a visiting quartet made a plea to the congregation not to be ashamed to return to their old songs, but to sing them again for the sake of their race. He himself had just come within an hour from the threshing field, he was one of them, one of the workers, and he spoke with power and authority. He pleaded with dignity and a lack of self-consciousness for the uplifting of their spirits. He carries weight because they know he is one of them, a tiller of the soil like them, an earnest, sincere man who is interested in the good of his people.

In this little nucleus of singing people is a noble spirit of which America should be proud.

What is an artist for? Certainly not to make the world more confused. If I can only convey to white people this sense that the power of God is really present here for us, people of all colors, then I will feel that my mission is accomplished.

[These religious songs] rank among the classic folk expressions in the whole world because of their moving simplicity, characteristic originality, and universal appeal. Although products of the slave era and the religious fervor of the plantation religion, they have outlived ... the conditions which produced them. They have lived through the contempt of the slave owners.

[These] are deeply religious songs. Right now in little remote churches all over the south, quartets are singing for the people, not for radio fame but for the simple Christian duty of helping souls to find heaven. These groups of singers are in deadly earnest and full of religious zeal. They come out of the wheat fields and tomato patches, right from the threshing, the crabhouse, oyster shucking, to sing for their own people. Very many of these quartets cannot read a note of music, yet [they are] so phenomenal in their musical sense that they make an orchestral harmony with savage, haunting undertones out of a simple song. The singing of these black Americans is one of the wonders of the new world.

'Strong, Determined Women'
Ruth Starr Rose found some success in her day. She won some prizes, got featured in some notable exhibits, had a solo show, and sold works to important museums. But after her death in 1965 she mostly dropped off the art world's radar screen. The big museums shuttled her works off into storage vaults. Her story

got lost as well. By the early 2000s even folks in Copperville had only a vague notion that this white socialite artist had joined their community and painted their grandparents, great aunts, and other ancestors.

Curator Barbara Paca has been key to reviving interest in Rose and her work. Paca is best known as a landscape architect. She has deep family roots on Maryland's Eastern Shore. She first stumbled into one of Rose's paintings sometime around 2004. When she encountered that portrait of Anna May Moaney, she was hooked. She took that painting to New York and showed it to her most trusted art world friends. Paca recalled their response in an article in Vassar College's alumni magazine.

This is a serious, serious painting, and a serious, serious artist.

What made it so special?

I think that's mainly because of an emotional bond that was created. Anna May Moaney, the sitter, is looking at Ruth, the artist, with total trust. There is mutual respect. She knows the person painting her isn't going to compromise her, not show her as a minstrel but show her for what she is, and what they both were: strong, determined women.

Paca went all in on collecting the works of Ruth Starr Rose. She found her way to a treasure trove of Rose's sketches and notes that had survived in near-miraculous fashion in the possession of a doorman in a New York City apartment building with ties to the Rose family. Eventually, Paca set out to reintroduce the people of Copperville to Ruth Starr Rose. One man who grew up there, Jeffrey Moaney, said this to the writer of that Vassar magazine piece:

I am proud, and I am touched. None of our family even knew these paintings existed until last year.

Then Paca set about reintroducing Ruth Starr Rose to the broader world. She helped put together a big exhibit in 2015 at the Reginald F. Lewis Museum of African American History in Baltimore, a show that then traveled to other locations. She helped spearhead the development and opening of the Water's Edge Museum in 2021. She wrote two books about the artist. And so, 50 years after her death, Ruth Starr Rose came back to metaphorical life.

'Lo, How Good and How Beautiful It Is'

Remember that mural Rose painted for Deshields Church in Copperville, the one focused on the parting of a Red Sea that came complete with a steamboat? The story of the unveiling of "Pharaoh's Army Got Drownd'd" returns us to where we started, with that unlikely-seeming invitation to "A Sacred Outing" on Miles River Neck. Here is Rose, as quoted in the book, "There Is a City Called Heaven:"

Installed at last in its place of honor above the pulpit and the Bible, it was unveiled with much ceremony, with singing and with ringing words of preaching, ennobled by the fine native dignity of the Negroes, In gratitude, the brethren of the church asked me if they could come to my house in June, when the honey locust is blooming by the tidewater and bring a chorus of 50 singers. The great day came; turning into a festival of white and colored for the benefit of the Copperville church. Choruses and quartets sang, and a young Negro preacher spoke, "Lo, how good and how beautiful it is for brethren to dwell together in unity."

Afternotes

• The Water's Edge Museum is located at 101 Mill St. in Oxford, Md.

• One of Barbara Paca's books about Ruth Starr Rose is *There Is a City Called Heaven: Songs of Strength by the Founding Black Families of Maryland*, which is based on Rose's notes and follows the plan for a book she hoped to put together in her lifetime. The other is the catalog book for Reginald F. Lewis Museum show: *Ruth Starr Rose (1887-1965): Revelations of African American Life in Maryland and the World*.

22 INGENUITY
BLACK VOTERS IN CHESTERTOWN OUTWIT THE ESTABLISHMENT, 1870

Politics these days got you down, with so many folks calling each other names? Yeah, me too. But I'm happy to report that there is a ray of hope to be found in Delmarva days gone by. Our modern political parties might learn a little something from the example of a happy, determined, and wonderfully clever batch of citizens who shocked everyone by winning an election in the Eastern Shore town of Chestertown, Md.

Pretty much everybody across the ages thinks, like we do today, that they live in unprecedented times. Truth be told, our country was more sharply and dangerously politically divided in 1870 than it is today. The Civil War had just ended. Abraham Lincoln had been murdered. Reconstruction times had dawned.

The spring of 1870 brought a bombshell development along the contentious political fault line of those times—race relations. The 15th Amendment had won approval in three-fourths of the states, and President Ulysses S. Grant announced that black men now had the right to vote.

177

This was not regarded as good news by most of Maryland's powerbrokers. Quite the opposite: The state was ruled by Democrats, a party that had mostly opposed the abolition of slavery. Now they were less than thrilled about seeing blacks getting a fuller measure of citizenship. Maryland hadn't just declined to ratify the black suffrage amendment: Incredibly, the state legislature had voted against it *unanimously*.

Those lawmakers regarded black men as too dumb and uneducated to deserve a voice in civic affairs. This sentiment was especially strong on the Eastern Shore, but the power brokers there would soon learn that their assumptions about black men were, well, dumb and uneducated.

A Slow Start for Suffrage

Early on the new amendment was a flop. The first post-amendment election to pop up—in Salisbury that April—saw a black vote total of ... zero. Next came an election in St. Michaels, where the black vote count was ... zero. Then came an election in Easton—same thing. The *Easton Star* newspaper summed that development up with what reads to my modern-day ears as a bit of happy sarcasm:

Africa did not make his appearance on the field of action.

Why the slow start? I haven't come across a crystal-clear explanation. Were black voters afraid to come out? Did they feel threatened? Were they uninformed about their new rights? One historian who looked into this, C. Christopher Brown, points to an anomaly in that Salisbury election. Only registered voters were allowed to cast ballots, but officials there hadn't bothered in advance of the election day to set up a process by which blacks could register.

Perhaps those officials didn't have enough time. That election happened just a few days after the amendment became law. But then again, everybody could see in advance that black suffrage was coming. Up in Chestertown, for instance, anti-black suffrage Democrats saw the writing on the wall—and prepared for it. Two years earlier, in 1868, they had sought and won permission from a friendly state legislature to restrict voting only to property owners.

News flash: Black property owners were few and far between in those days.

'Victory Crowned the Act'
But black property owners were *not* nonexistent. Chestertown had a healthy handful of successful black businessmen. William Perkins's Rising Sun oyster saloon was a dining destination known all over the Eastern Shore. James Jones ran a successful grocery store. They used profits from those businesses to buy some land, as did a man named Isaac Anderson (I haven't been able to figure out how Anderson made his money).

But most blacks in Chestertown worked as servants or unskilled laborers. Small businessmen who ran barber shops or harvested oysters did a little better, but rarely better enough to make real money and buy property.

This is not a story where I am building up suspense toward a surprise ending. Chestertown became the first Eastern Shore town where black voters turned out in big numbers— enough to decide an election. The *Baltimore American* newspaper:

A new era has dawned on the people of Chestertown. The colored man has cast his ballot for the first time, and victory crowned the act.

How did Chestertown turn that trick where other, similarly situated towns had failed so miserably? Chalk it up to a one-two-three combination of generosity, community-minded fun, and legal ingenuity. Nearly every newly eligible black voter turned out on May 23, 1870, thanks to a campaign by well-off black civic leaders that C. Christopher Brown says nurtured a "remarkable sense of patriotism and citizenship" among their poorer neighbors.

That first punch, generosity, came courtesy of those business owners who could have sat on their plump nest eggs. Instead, they sank time and money into building community enthusiasm for voting rights. Almost before the ink had dried on President Ulysses S. Grant's signature on the amendment, Perkins and Jones organized a rally at the town's biggest black church, Janes United Methodist.

Five hundred people packed the tabernacle for a night of speeches, preaching, and singing to celebrate the new law. About 100 white "Party of Lincoln" Republicans were in that crowd, too, showing support.

A few weeks later these black businessmen transitioned into part two of the strategy, fun. Just before election day they organized a parade and made a joyous civic racket. Excitement ran so high that the streets started filling up more than three hours before the noontime event. The *Baltimore Sun*:

The procession was composed of all sorts, sizes, colors, and descriptions of vehicles, filled with a mass of humanity attired in their best.

Schoolchildren waved the flags of every state in the union. The queen of the parade dressed as the Goddess of Liberty. There were 250 wagons, 300 mounted horsemen, and marching bands from as far away as Wilmington, Del.

After the parade marchers headed to a grove in Baker's Woods outside of town to enjoy an hours-long round of "singing, praying, political speaking, and the devouring of confectionery." When the party died down, the procession re-formed, everyone parading raucously back into town as dusk descended. The *Baltimore American* newspaper:

No similar celebration was ever witnessed in Chestertown. In respectability of numbers, manliness of deportment, neatness of dress, and citizen-like bearing, they challenged the admiration and respect of all good men in the community.

Chestertown's black population at this time numbered about 800, about 40 percent of the town. Some of you might well be raising an eyebrow at this point, considering how I said earlier that Chestertown had restricted voting only to property owners. That brings us to the third punch, legal ingenuity.

Before the election Isaac Anderson—the third of the black landowners I mentioned earlier, the one I haven't found much background on—filed a deed with officials in the offices of Kent County. A strange affair, this document covered a tiny plot of worthless land covering three feet, nine inches of marshy muck on the shores of the Chester River. Anderson's paperwork documented the sale of that sliver for $15 to a partnership that consisted of 44 black men.

Have you guessed? That law Chestertown passed in 1868 to restrict voting rights to property owners didn't specify how much land made a male property owner eligible to vote. This ingenious stunt played a big part in the shocking electoral victory of Lincoln Republicans, who made a clean sweep of all seven elective offices on the ballot.

The average margin of victory in those races was 22 votes, which means that those 44 co-owners of three feet, nine inches of worthless land made all the difference. When Anderson's land shenanigans became public knowledge, the losers reacted with outrage. The *Chestertown Democrat* newspaper:

[It was] a piece of as flagrant fraud as was ever devised.

The paper called for a criminal investigation. But the outraged losers had a big problem in making such a case. A group of their fellow white Democrats had pulled the same trick—albeit on a smaller scale—the year before. The beneficiaries of that trickery—involving three feet of worthless land along an alleyway—included several prominent white men, including the pastors of the biggest Episcopal and Methodist churches in town.

All Isaac Anderson and his neighbors had done was run through the same loophole in the law those white men of the cloth had used. Here is how the *Cecil Whig* newspaper summed up the losers' predicament:

This law was evidently an invention of the [Democrats] to keep poor men from the ballot, but finding the colored men had out-generaled them on their own ground, the leaders hauled down their old black flag of prejudice and hate.

Anderson and his compatriots had not committed a crime—and they were never charged with one. In fact, they doubled down on their cleverness, with another of the black property owners in town, James Jones, selling a single square foot of land the next year to a partnership of 50 black men.

News of the ingenuity of Chestertown's black community in that 1870 election spread like wildfire around the country. Republican-leaning newspapers here, there, and everywhere reprinted a story that first appeared in the *New York Tribune*. That story is what folks in Jackson, Ohio read in their local *Standard* newspaper:

The negroes of Maryland are showing themselves very apt scholars in the political school. Although so very recently enfranchised, they already appear to be almost as smart at little political games as white folks.

"Almost as smart?" That seems an understatement.

23 INTERLUDE
UNDERESTIMATING A 'PLAIN BOY IN RURAL LIFE'

I did not think as I might of what may be the manhood ... [ahead for] a plain boy in rural life on a farm.

L.T. Travers of Taylors Island, Md. confessed to that mistake as an old man, while recalling a childhood friendship. His apology is worth applying today as a general life rule, but perhaps especially when we pass by a couple of oddball-looking kids working the water's edge with fishing poles or crab nets.

Such scenes are still common along the backroads of the Delmarva Peninsula, just as they were in the 1840s when a boy named John Fletcher Hurst was growing up in Dorchester County, Md. Despite suffering from debilitating bouts of asthma, young John loved crabbing, fishing, and hunting every bit as much as his healthier friends. He would brag later in life about the bird traps he made, the fishing nets he wove, and the double-barreled shotgun he fired while its butt was propped on a friend's shoulder because neither of them was big enough to hold it at arm's length.

John grew up on a farm east of Cambridge, a little way beyond where the Hyatt resort stands today, but he spent a good amount of time, too, in the marshy remoteness west of Cambridge, especially on Taylors Island. That's where he met L.T. Travers, the man behind the apologetic quote above. The quote dates to 1894, with Travers recalling a scene he witnessed in the mid-1800s.

A 12-year-old boy is walking to church on Taylors Island alongside his father. An older sister was likely there as well. This trio's situation is complicated. The father has been a widower for five years. The boy worships the memory of his mother. But time passes and life goes on: John's father is now "paying attention" to a Taylors Island woman who would soon become his second wife, a "woman of Christian character who took deep and kind interest" in John and his older sister, Sallie.

John is decked out in what passes for his Sunday best, a plain brown suit. In manners and appearance he looks like any other local kid brought up amid the "simple and hearty ways and open hospitality" of the rural Eastern Shore. Travers felt a measure of pity at the sight of that asthmatic, motherless country boy in the plain suit. He never imagined that boy might grow into a man capable of big things.

I was but a youth then, myself, and it did not enter my thought that [John] was to be a great man in the church and a bishop. Perhaps I did not think as I might of what may be the manhood ... [ahead for] a plain boy in rural life on a farm.

But John Fletcher Hurst had a couple of invisible things going for him. First, the cherished memory of his birth mother. Second, a commitment to labor in faith. These were interconnected. From *John Fletcher Hurst: A Biography*, by Albert Osborn:

Ordinary Heroes of Old Delmarva

[That mother] left to her only boy the rich legacy of a mother's prayer. He carried with him to the end of life much of her disposition, temperament, manner, and resemblance in his features. ... His pen formed a beautiful tribute to her when mature in life: "If there is anything immortal in this world it is a mother's prayer. Her face, by a spiritual photography, is graven in the soul."

John Fletcher Hurst (1834-1903) went off to college and became a minister in the Methodist Episcopal church. Early in that career he wrote to a friend, describing what seems a modest mission statement:

I do not know what sort of place I shall get—perhaps a circuit, perhaps a little station. The Lord can do with me as he pleases. I am in His hands and [will] try to be willing to labor in whatever place He pleases.

What He pleased was for Hurst to leave footprints in the sand of time that folks are still walking today, more than a century after his passing. He got sent overseas to study and teach in Germany, which at the time ranked as the higher education gold standard of the Western world. Later he served as president of the Drew Theological Seminary in New Jersey and dug that institution out of a financial crisis that threatened its existence. Thanks to Hurst, it's still going strong in the 21st century.

He was promoted to bishop after that. In his later years Bishop Hurst would serve as the prime mover and shaker behind the founding of American University in Washington, D.C. He became such a renowned figure in his church—and around the country—that writers started showing up back in Dorchester County, tracking down locals like L.T. Travers and asking them about that poor, asthmatic, motherless country boy, the one he never imagined might grow up to make waves in the world.

24 WISDOM
THE WHALEYVILLE WONDER MAKES A DIFFERENCE IN THE WORLD

What was Dale Wimbrow thinking on that day in 1934 when he picked up a pen and set words to paper? He could not have known in that moment that in the decades to follow his words would spread like an inspirational inferno, giving strength to hundreds, thousands, millions of men and women. Those words are still doing good works today—in pretty much every corner of the globe.

While researching Wimbrow's life I had a fleeting and somewhat irreverent thought: What if he was just going through the motions that day? It would be understandable. By that point Wimbrow was a falling star, no longer a musical sensation with a nationwide audience. His days of hosting shows on the biggest radio station in the land were in the past. Journalists weren't knocking at his door anymore to do human-interest stories about the happy-go-lucky rising star from Whaleyville, Md. with a round face and his messy mop of strawberry-blond hair.

Wimbrow had started doing the sorts of things that falling

stars do. In modern times that might mean cheesy bits on reality TV and game shows. In the 1930s it meant joining a panel of celebrities put together by *The American* magazine to give advice to readers.

One assignment: Reply to a poignant, touching letter from a young girl. She had seen her father—a decent, upstanding man—get cheated, mistreated, and humiliated in life. Why, the girl asked, should she bother striving to live in that same decent, upstanding way?

Wimbrow's Words Go Wild

The day came. Wimbrow sat down to write. Did he use a pen or a typewriter? Did he need to noodle around on his beloved ukulele to get his thoughts straight?

What he came up with was a little ditty of a poem. After it appeared in the magazine, someone, somewhere took his words to heart. That someone shared the verses with a neighbor. That neighbor mailed his words to a relative. That relative put the ditty on display in the office.

So it went. On and on and on. From town to town, state to state, and country to country. Year after year. Decade after decade. Wimbrow's words went this way and that, hither and yon, crossing oceans and mountain ranges. They ended up in corporate boardrooms, on church bulletin boards, in self-help manuals, behind ornate frames, crumpled up in wallets, in high school oratory contests, and—especially, most especially—at meetings of Alcoholics Anonymous. The AA transformed Wimbrow's ditty into a lifeline, sharing his words with new arrivals as if to say:

Here is a good place to start thinking about your new one-day-at-a-time life.

189

Weird thing, though. As Wimbrow's words went meandering around the world they got detached from the name of the author. Often the poem was credited to "Anonymous." There were countless other contenders, too. A schoolteacher from Louisiana. A public relations guy from Avon. A recovering drunk in Colorado. A cult rock band out of Detroit. The saddest bit of attribution I came across was to an unnamed dead drug addict whose mother supposedly was so embarrassed by her son's fatal weakness that she refused to share his name.

Pretty much everybody and anybody got credit, except for the happy-go-lucky guy from Whaleyville. Let's go back and meet him, shall we? His journey through life raises lots of interesting questions:

• How much does it matter—or should it matter—whether we get credit for good deeds?

• How should we react when long-term health problems or other setbacks ruin our best-laid plans in life?

• How did a white boy from Whaleyville who grew up in segregation times end up thinking that a benefit concert he did for a black church outside that town ranked as perhaps the most memorable night of his life?

• What role, if any, did Wimbrow's near-death experiences play in shaping his life?

Of Childhood Mysteries and Poison Gas
Peter Dale Wimbrow came into the world on June 6, 1895.

Ordinary Heroes of Old Delmarva

Whaleyville had a population of 258 then. It's closer to 150 today. If you're headed to Ocean City, Md. along Route 50, Whaleyville is one in a run of small towns east of Salisbury: Parsonsburg, Pittsville, Willards, then Whaleyville. The next time you're about to zoom by, take a minute to pull off the highway and give the town a look. According to the Maryland Historical Trust, the architectural and geographical landscape of Dale Wimbrow's childhood is still very much in evidence:

Few modern intrusions have altered the nineteenth-century village character.

Timbering had been the center of economic activity in Whaleyville for many decades as Wimbrow came into the world, but that era was coming to a close. The last of the good trees in the area would be cleared and harvested by the time of the First World War.

Dale's father, who had the glorious first name of Nutter, was a serial entrepreneur. After moving to Whaleyville from Salisbury, Nutter Wimbrow opened a general store, launched a sawmill, started a basket-making company, and built a cannery. Nutter also built a good reputation for himself—he ended up winning election at one point to the state House of Delegates.

It must have been somewhere in these childhood years that Dale latched onto music as a life passion, but I don't know when or how that happened. Wimbrow's younger years are mostly a blank slate in the historical record, all the way up to the point where he dropped out of Western Maryland College to sign up for the army just after World War I broke out in 1917.

He ended up overseas in the midst of the Meuse-Argonne Forest Offensive, the largest, bloodiest encounter of that notori-

191

ously brutal war. From a newspaper profile of Wimbrow written decades after the war:

[Dale Wimbrow's] closest call with the inevitable Reaper was in the Argonne Forest during the First World War. Seriously wounded and gassed, he was consigned to [an] ambulance which, in the confusion [of the battle scene], drove off without him. Hours later, [while in another ambulance], he rumbled past what was left of [that first] ambulance: it had been blown to bits.

Wimbrow eventually got back on his feet, but that mustard gas would stay in his body and wreak a lot of havoc in later years. In his 30s it caused throat problems that brought his singing career to a premature close. In his 40s it led to eyesight issues that short-circuited fledgling second careers in painting and photography. There's no telling whether the gas was involved in his death from a heart attack at the age of 58.

From Backroads to Broadway Lights
Like most "overnight" sensations, Dale Wimbrow worked his tail off for years before bursting onto the national music scene. After returning from World War I he had day jobs as a traveling salesman and a civil engineer, playing club gigs and appearing in vaudeville stage shows by night. The ukulele was his favorite instrument. (Later, when he was a big star, he would invent the "Wimbrola," a six-string alternative to the ukulele that had a "mellower" sound.) He became a national name at about the age of 30, in 1925. Here is the *Baltimore Sun* that year:

One of these Maryland boys, a red-headed chap weighing about 200 pounds, seeped into New York last week and pretty near conquered the playgoing world. ... He shook off some of the dust of Whaleyville ... to sing some of his ukulele ditties up in the big town.

That story contained the news that Wimbrow had signed a recording contract. Plus, a theatrical producer had his eye on Wimbrow for a recurring role on one of the biggest vaudeville revues in the Big Apple. To readers outside Delmarva this part of the story probably looked like it happened in the blink of an eye, a lucky break. Here is Wimbrow, recounting some of the barnstorming that led up to his big break.

Having no money [to travel], we took [our new song] around the Shore. ... We packed Lee Insley's Arcade Theater [in Salisbury] three nights in a row. Believe me, ... that was big time for this Whaleyviller with hay in his hair. We did well in Princess Anne— even Chincoteague, Virginia. We did a "land office" box office until we [got to] Whaleyville. We felt that we must by all means include the good old hometown in the itinerary. So we did. When it came time to roll up the curtain we gave a peep out and how many people were in the audience, do you think? There were eight people, including the dog under the stove. I don't remember ever feeling more humiliated.

By the time he wrote those words Wimbrow could afford to laugh about such nights. In the late 1920s he recorded for Columbia and Decca, two of the best and biggest labels in the land. He was standing front and center on New York City stages, performing for crowds that included the biggest celebrities of his day. Best of all, right around this same time, he met and married his true love, a radio-show writer named Dorothy Livezy. The great Rudy Vallee and his orchestra played at their nuptials.

During that musical heyday Dale Wimbrow went by several different nicknames. Sometimes he was "The Del-Mar-Va Songster." Down South he was "The Mississippi Minstrel." With tongue in cheek he claimed the title of "Outstanding Loafer of the Good Old Eastern Shore." That last one is a reference to one of his best-known songs, "The Good Old Eastern Shore."

Big Star with a Big Heart
We've all read about people who get big heads after becoming stars, but that doesn't seem to have happened to Dale Wimbrow. At the height of his fame Wimbrow often took time to pitch in for good causes. In 1924 he donated proceeds from a new song to benefit the W. Freeland Kendrick Convalescent Home for Crippled Children in Philadelphia. The song, "Sunshine," includes these lyrics:

After the darkest hours
Then comes the break of day
So never grieve
But try to believe
The storm clouds will roll away.

The year 1926 was peak stardom for Wimbrow. The nation's biggest radio station, WJZ in New York City, did a series of six shows that year called "The Del-Mar-Va Hour" that showcased regional talent and culture. Sponsored by a marketing cooperative made up of Eastern Shore businesses, it had Wimbrow as star attraction and "The Good Old Eastern Shore" as a theme song. Later, Wimbrow joked that the show helped turn that song into such a big hit that only two people in America had yet to hear it:

One is deaf and the other has no radio.

During this period Wimbrow commuted regularly between the Lower Eastern Shore and New York City. I spoke at one point in my research with Vaughn Baker, a 12th-generation Eastern Shoreman. He told me how his father, Harry Baker, often drove Wimbrow up to Wilmington, Del., where the singer would then catch a train. The two were drinking buddies, Baker added.

Wimbrow's recording contract at that time required him to deliver a new song every week. According to Baker family legend Wimbrow often spent the drive to Wilmington frantically composing a new tune on deadline. It's fun to think about how some of his songs were written while riding shotgun along the backroads of Delmarva.

At some point during that busy year of 1926 Wimbrow returned home to do a benefit concert to raise funds to build an addition for Pullet's Chapel, the black church in Whaleyville. This did not come as a big surprise during my research, despite the segregation ethos of those times. I had already come across an article that referred to the way Wimbrow wrote songs patterned after "negro spirituals." I had already started to wonder whether the black community in Whaleyville had played an important role in his musical upbringing.

Later in life Wimbrow wrote an essay about the night of his Pullet's Chapel benefit show.

They came from Parsonsburg in buses, and Jenkins Neck in Carry-alls. They came in Packards, one-lung jalopies, and ox carts. They were packed fifty deep outside ... and inside, it would have taken a hydraulic press to pack 'em in tighter.

He claims in that essay that the raucous, overflow crowd at Pullets inspired him to play perhaps the best and most satisfying show of his career.

Finally, limp and wet with the sweat of fatigue I had to sign off. ... I shall never forget that night.

Life on the road as a musician—and later, a move to Florida—would keep Dale Wimbrow away from his beloved Delmarva Peninsula for long stretches as the years went on. But he always held the place close to his heart. In a 1938 book, *The Eastern Shore (of Maryland) in Song and Story*, writer W.C. Thurston had this to say:

If you talk to Dale about the Eastern Shore his voice gets husky; he's a sentimental cuss. .... If you deride the Shore his face gets red, and to continue at any length would be dangerous. ... He is just as lovable as the Shore itself. ... He's got that Eastern Sho' way about him that makes you like him whether you want to or not. He's the Shore's own son, and never—nowhere, has he ever been ashamed to own her cause.

Falling Star: What To Do When Stardom Goes South?
The successes and the accolades kept on coming for a while. Wimbrow's name appeared frequently in newspapers up and down the Eastern Seaboard, through the Deep South, and into the Midwest. One of his songs, "Accordion Joe," got covered by Duke Ellington. I've seen numerous reports that Judy Garland recorded another of his songs, though I haven't been able to track that one down.

Ordinary Heroes of Old Delmarva

He continued playing music through the 1930s, but his
popularity waned as his singing voice lost ground in its battle
with the long-term effects of that mustard gas he'd inhaled in the
Argonne Forest during World War I.

Dale and Dorothy Wimbrow had two children, Salliedale
and Peter. Salliedale grew up to become a realtor in Florida. A
community newspaper there did a routine "Focus on Seniors"
feature story about her when she was 70 years old, in 1998. In
that interview Salliedale recalled the itinerant years of her childhood by saying that she attended 24 different schools in the 1930s
while her father chased an endless parade of radio shows, vaudeville gigs, and concert tours. Basically, Salliedale wrote:

I grew up in the back seat of a car.

You can get a sense in the old newspapers that Dale Wimbrow
knew the end was nigh for his singing career. Perhaps he looked
to his serial entrepreneur of a father for inspiration. He launched
a line of hand-crafted walking sticks and canes, made from exotic
woods and featuring handles in the shape of ibises and other creatures. Wimbrow tried his hand at oil painting and photography,
but then the mustard gas started taking a toll on his eyesight.

The health-status hammer really came down in 1939. Both
Wimbrow children remember how the family's move to Florida
as a dark time. A doctor had predicted their father would die soon,
probably within six months. That doctor recommended a warmer
climate. They tried Miami for a while, but quickly migrated up
the Atlantic Coast a bit, to a rural area outside of Sebastian known
as Indian River.

Those six months came and went. Then a year. Then more
years. Dale Wimbrow stopped waiting on that death sentence and

jumped back into action. In the late 1940s he crawled out on a limb with a new business venture. The way he recalls that start-up happening makes it sound like a reprise of those penniless early days of barnstorming through Delmarva with his ukulele.

My wife was off visiting in Key West, and as usual when the ol' cat was away, this mouse played. ... I went into business establishments and said just this: "I'm going to start a newspaper [for the communities] along the Indian River. ... If you feel like coming along, give me four weeks [of] advertising [money] in advance and we'll publish for at least a month. If I can't make it go, I'll send your money back to you." So help me, the merchants handed over the advertising money.

When my wife got off the train and said, "And what have you been doing since I've been out of sight?" I answered, "We've done got us a newspaper."

'The Guy in the Glass'
One Dale Wimbrow quote stands out here in my mind. It's not from one of his songs, but from a few thoughts he shared about that final professional chapter of his, as a newspaperman:

Perhaps the Indian River News isn't that important, but it still puts words down in black and white [and] words are powerful things.

That brings us back to our starting point, that day in 1934 when *The American* magazine asked falling star Dale Wimbrow to respond to that young girl who had doubts about whether she should lead an upstanding, honest life.

Ordinary Heroes of Old Delmarva

Wimbrow's reply was titled "The Guy in the Glass."

When you get what you want in your struggle for pelf,
And the world makes you King for a day,
Then go to the mirror and look at yourself,
And see what that guy has to say.

For it isn't your Father, or Mother, or Wife,
Who judgment upon you must pass.
The feller whose verdict counts most in your life
Is the guy staring back from the glass.

He's the feller to please, never mind all the rest,
For he's with you clear up to the end,
And you've passed your most dangerous, difficult test
If the guy in the glass is your friend.

You may be like Jack Horner and "chisel" a plum,
And think you're a wonderful guy,
But the man in the glass says you're only a bum
If you can't look him straight in the eye.

You can fool the whole world down the pathway of years,
And get pats on the back as you pass,
But your final reward will be heartaches and tears
If you've cheated the guy in the glass.

Perhaps you've come across this poem in your life's journey.
God knows that's true for millions upon millions of people. As
I mentioned it's a staple with the Alcoholics Anonymous crowd.
Super Bowl-winning football coach Bill Parcells recited the poem

at his retirement press conference. The poem became a big deal in England when soccer coach Nigel Adkins recited it from memory after his Southampton Football Club lost a tough match to an archrival.

"The Guy in the Glass" has been read into the Congressional Record—several times, in fact. It was put to raucous 1960s garage-band music by a cult band from Detroit, The Underdogs.

Dale Wimbrow was still alive to see his poem start spreading here and there, hither and yon. It bothered him, the way he rarely got credit for the words. It angered him when people tried to claim his words as their own. In 1947 Wimbrow filed a lawsuit against an author from Catonsville, Md. who had included "The Guy in the Glass" in a book in a way that made it look like he, not Wimbrow, had written the poem.

But he never succeeded in his efforts to get credited as the author of "The Guy in the Glass." Neither did his children, who kept up the campaign after Wimbrow's death. That battle was finally won in 1983 thanks to Ann Landers, the famed advice columnist whose work appeared in newspapers all over the country. In October of that year she published "The Guy in the Glass" and attributed it to a dead drug addict. Letters poured in claiming she had gotten that authorship wrong, that someone else wrote the poem. But there was a problem: Every letter she received offered up a different name as the true and rightful author.

Landers and her staff dug through all the candidates and figured it out. She published a follow-up the next month, thanking Peter Wimbrow for his help and confirming to the world once and for all that the poem had indeed been written by Peter's father. Peter and his sister would later put up a ramshackle website devoted to "The Guy in the Glass." Still trying to set the record straight about authorship, here is what one of them wrote:

[Our father's words have] touched the souls of millions of people the world over. ... [He] was the most gifted and caring person we ever knew.... He would have wanted his work to be a gift and so do we. All we ask is that you properly credit him somewhere in your publication as the author.

The Final, Prayerful Days of Dale Wimbrow
The newspaper life in South Florida wasn't anything like the bright lights of New York City, but Dale Wimbrow made a nice name for himself in the Sunshine State. His paper won several awards for journalistic excellence. The best of his essays and editorials on local affairs were collected into a book, *Swamp Cabbage and Angel Wings*. In his mind the big picture looked like this:

The [rewards] in money are not great. [But] it is a living, and as such, I am grateful.

From his perch as a small-town celebrity Wimbrow also got the opportunity to do some public speaking. He addressed church groups, women's clubs, and veterans' associations. His talks usually focused on how timeless Christian values should play out in the modern world. Faith is a big part of Wimbrow's story, too. Here is a childhood memory shared by his son, Peter:

I remember as a young boy watching him, as he did every night of his life, get down on his knees by the bed and in silent reverence, with his hands clasped, say his prayers.

There is no telling for sure how much that faith had to do with

Dale Wimbrow's ability to bounce back in life, time and again, whether reaching for the stars as a young man or while reinventing himself several times after his star dimmed and various plans went awry.

On Jan. 23, 1954 Dale Wimbrow was on stage speaking to an American Legion gathering in Vero Beach when he suffered a heart attack and collapsed. He died three days later, at the age of 58. His body was returned home to a resting place in the Dale cemetery in Whaleyville. If you're ever passing through Roseland, Fla., maybe stop and take a break at Dale Wimbrow Park?

Here's hoping and trusting that Dale Wimbrow was ready to look the man in the mirror square in the eye on his way out of this world.

Afternote: A Trio of Wimbrow Tidbits
• The word at the end of the first line of "The Guy in the Glass" really is *pelf*. If you look it up you will see that it means "money, especially when gained in a dishonest or dishonorable way."

• Among the Wimbrow song titles you should search for on the internet if you're interested in fun, scratchy old recordings: "The Good Old Eastern Shore," "When Old Pete Daley Plays His Ukelele Down in Whaleyville," "The County Fair in Delaware," "Country Bred and Chicken Fed," and "It Takes a Good Woman (to Keep a Good Man at Home)."

• Local musicians Louise Anderson and Diana Wagner have done wonderful work keeping the music of Dale Wimbrow alive. If you ever get a chance to see their two-woman show of Wimbrow songs, don't miss it. Both have had long professional connections with Salisbury University—Anderson as an assistant professor of music and Wagner as an associate professor of education. They co-wrote a wonderful article about Wimbrow's music in the 2023 issue of *Maryland Historical* magazine.

25 COURAGE
THE HELICOPTER HERO OF '62 THROWS CAUTION TO THE WIND

By March 7, 1962, the so-called Ash Wednesday storm had battered the Delaware coast for 24-plus hours, with two or three more days of the same in the forecast. Floodwaters rising. Gale-force winds whipping. Before petering out the storm would kill 40 people, injure more than a thousand, and trash hundreds of millions of dollars in property.

The men working at the Indian River Inlet Coast Guard Station near Bethany Beach had been through bad storms before, but even they were caught off guard by how fast and furiously the tide rolled in that day. They decided to evacuate, wading through chest-high waters. They reached an island of nearby sand still poking up over the water, but how long did they have before the seas covered that island, too?

They had no idea. Best guess: Not long.

'I Had the Helicopter, and [Those Men] Had to Get Out'
Word of their plight reached a Delaware National Guard unit

stationed at the little airport in Rehoboth Beach. Big problem: The only helicopter there was a Bell H-13. Designed in the 1940s the H-13 was on its last legs as a military tool by this point. It was small—just two cramped seats, one for a pilot and one for a passenger. Making matters worse: Safety protocols rated it unsafe at wind speeds over 35 miles per hour.

The gales of the Ash Wednesday storm were up over 50, gusts reaching 70 and 80. A supervisor asked if any pilots on duty would be willing to throw caution to the wind and volunteer. James Sulpizi stepped up. Later, the 33-year-old from New Castle would describe that decision in nothing-to-see-here, matter-of-fact language.

I had the helicopter, and [those stranded men] had to get out.

He and his colleagues at the airport came up with a plan to try and boost the stability of the H-13. Before taking off Sulpizi would load three 25-pound bags full of buckshot onto the passenger seat, providing a child-sized extra measure of ballast for the nine-mile flight from the airport to the five stranded men.

After arriving at the sandbar, Sulpizi would throw those bags of buckshot into the tail and let one man climb into that lone passenger seat. He'd fly back to Rehoboth and start the process over again. Each round trip took 40 minutes.

During his first or second trip Sulpizi noted something that wasn't on his to-do list. Five stranded National Guardsmen looked to be in even more peril than the station crew. They were clinging to the top of trucks that were rocking this way and that in the waves.

Figuring that those station crew members would survive on their island for a little longer, he turned his attention to the truck clingers. Here, Sulpizi would land on a nearby spit of sand. One of the men would tie a long rope around his body—the other end was attached to the truck—and wade out to the helicopter through chin-high floodwaters.

Sulpizi rescued all five of those guys. Two didn't know how to swim.

Then he turned his attention back to the Coast Guard station. He made 10 trips in all, over the course of six or seven hours. Every takeoff was treacherous, every landing a windswept nightmare. Sulpizi finally got to give that H-13 a rest once a bigger and better helicopter arrived from Fort Meade over on the western shore of Maryland.

The Distinguished Flying Cross
Four months later, on July 6, Sulpizi would become the first Delaware guardsman to earn a Distinguished Flying Cross, the highest honor our nation bestows upon military men and women for peacetime heroism. The award was made in Bethany Beach, where the townsfolk put on a parade in his honor. Here are a couple of highlights from the declaration signed by President John F. Kennedy:

During a disastrous storm and flood that struck the Delaware coast, Captain Sulpizi unhesitatingly volunteered to fly the only available aircraft, a one-passenger H-13 helicopter to rescue personnel in danger of drowning from rising flood waters at the Indian River Coast Guard Station.

With complete disregard for his own personal safety, and by skill-fully piloting his aircraft through violent atmospheric turbulence that normally would preclude all flight operations, he coura-

geously made ten round-trip rescue missions of approximately nine miles each way. Although gale-force winds rendered the operation of the small helicopter extremely hazardous, he successfully rescued five persons from the Coast Guard Station. By continuing in his efforts, he evacuated five other victims who were clinging to trucks awash in the treacherous floodwaters.

Captain Sulpizi's strong determination, presence of mind, and heroic action in this emergency saved the lives of ten persons [and] reflect great credit on himself and military service.

In the years that followed Sulpizi enjoyed an illustrious career as a pilot and teacher, eventually earning quite a nickname, "The Father of Aviation" in the Delaware Army National Guard. He retired in 1984. He passed away in 2017 at the age of 83.

26 COMMUNITY
TURNING ORPHANS INTO
'POOR LITTLE RICH GIRLS'

The skies threatened heavy snow on the chilly November day in 1868 when Anna Earle lost control of her emotions. What, exactly, set her off? She must have seen something. A small boy, shivering in a farm field, perhaps, or a little girl with a lost and helpless look.

Whatever it was, it sent Earle into a state of frenzied urgency. She had to do something, anything, swing into action, right this second. But what? She had no idea. Maybe her friend Mrs. Dawson would know! Despite the snow in the air Earle hitched the horses up to her carriage and set out on a solo drive from her home in the town of Queen Anne, headed 15 miles away to Easton.

Elias Dawson was outside when his wife's friend pulled up to his house at Washington and Bay streets.

What on earth brings you here in this kind of weather? Well never mind. It must be important!

Elias took charge of Earle's carriage and horses. Inside, his wife fired up some coffee. Mrs. Dawson saw straight away that her friend was on edge.

All right Anna. Out with it!

First up, a funny misunderstanding. Somehow, Mrs. Dawson guessed that her friend—a longtime "spinster"—was about to announce her engagement.

Who's the lucky man? Why have you kept this secret?

Not even close. Earle was closer to heartbroken, though not over a man. What had brought her to Mrs. Dawson's home was the sadness and outrage she felt over a social issue—the care of orphan children. You know, kids like in Oliver Twist. That Charles Dickens novel that had been published just a few decades before.
    Let's put Anna Earle's meltdown in historical perspective.

• Too many orphans lived on Maryland's Eastern Shore in the late 1860s. Fathers had died in the Civil War. A post-war smallpox epidemic added to the toll of lost parents.

• Single parents faced daunting obstacles. Who would care for kids while a father was at work? How would a mother make money in an era when job opportunities for women were hard to come by?

• Some widows and widowers pulled it off, but many others landed in desperate straits, forced to give up some or all their children.

• What to do, exactly? There were no orphanages on the Eastern

Shore. Nor was there a modern-day foster care system.

• Some parents managed to place children with relatives or neighbors, but others faced heart-wrenching choices. Some "abandoned" children ended up in almshouses, facilities that housed desperately poor and, often, mentally ill adults. Not an ideal atmosphere for child rearing.

• Other "abandoned" children ended up in "apprenticeships" on the farms of strangers. The farmers agreed to provide food and shelter, but the kids were expected to earn their keep by working fields or toiling as servants. Some kids were treated fairly, but many others were not—sleeping in barns or shacks, clad in tattered clothes, eating starvation rations, working ungodly hours. None of these kids went to school.

This is the problem Anna Earle dropped in Mrs. Dawson's lap over coffee. The hostess sympathized. She could even attach the name of a specific boy to the tragedy—George Todd, an eight-year-old "apprentice" she thought of as "the dearest boy." But he "did not even have a decent pair of shoes." Instead, he was heading into the winter months wearing pieces of quilt, tied with leather straps, on his feet.

    The two women traded horror stories—kids sleeping four or five to a single corn husk mattress, that kind of thing. Earle tried to put things in an understanding perspective.

The farmers mean well and really deserve a lot of credit for taking [in] the orphans in exchange for their keep. They should, however, work out a plan to send the children to school instead of keeping them at chores from sunup to sunset.

The conversation petered out, no solutions in sight. At least Earle had gotten the orphan business off her chest. She left with this thought in her head:

God would show her the way.

That's pretty much what happened. Fast forward a few months, to a Sunday in April 1869. Earle was in a pew at Christ Episcopal Church. A newly arrived prelate, Bishop Henry Champlin Lay, built his sermon around a familiar Bible line.

In as much as ye do it unto the least of these my brethren, you have done it unto me.

Remember the old Hollywood musical, "Babes in Arms?" The moment when young Mickey Rooney goes wild-eyed with inspiration?

Let's put on a show!

A lightbulb went off in Earle's head.

Let's build an orphanage!

She was not thinking about one of those dreary *Oliver Twist* prisons for children. She was thinking about a newfangled kind of orphanage that was just then coming into vogue in America, based on holistic child-rearing ideas that would become the foundation of our modern notions of child welfare. These new orphanages strived to create a loving environment. They aimed to promote education, careers, and Christian morals. Earle had probably heard about a couple of brand new facilities in big-city Baltimore that were starting to put those ideas into practice.

Five ladies had tea with the bishop a few days later. Many more teas followed. A plan emerged, then a constitution, then a board of directors. The Episcopal diocese came up with some money. The state government agreed to pitch in. The people of Easton embraced the project. So did other towns, as they learned that the proposed orphanage would serve the whole of Maryland's Eastern Shore.

When it became known ... that a project was underway to provide a home for little children, the town [of Easton] felt a glow of pride. Women discussed [it] while hanging clothes in backyards. It was the chief subject at teas, church meetings, and wherever people gathered. Circuit-riding preachers, not only of the Episcopal faith but of others as well, carried the news to outlying regions. Salesmen and peddlers also played a big part in telling the back-country folk.

The board cobbled together $5,000, about $120,000 in modern dollars. That was enough to buy a home on Glebe Road. The building was too small. It needed work. It was too far from the center of town. But it was cheap, and it came with 46 acres of land that could be rented to farmers, generating revenue.

As this news spread folks in Easton and lots of other towns started cleaning out closets, boxing up clothes, sheets, and toys for donation. Volunteers showed up to make repairs, hang curtains, mop floors, and paint rooms.

Anna Earle's dream came true on Jan. 13, 1871. Brace yourself: The place had a name on opening day that will sound like a nightmare to modern-day ears:

The Home for Friendless Children on the Eastern Shore.

Among the first two residents was that "dearest boy" Mrs. Dawson had fretted about, George Todd. He and another child pulled up to the house in a carriage driven by Bishop Lay.

The children hopped lightly down from the carriage and just as they did that a playful gust of wind dislodged fluffs of snow from a low hanging branch. [The snow] covered both children. Merrily, they laughed carefree laughter, happy children coming into their own. Thus it was that the doors opened ... on a note of gaiety.

Friendless No More: George and Norma

Those doors stayed open for an amazing 87 years, until 1958. Lots of changes unfolded in those decades. The orphanage eventually adopted a less depressing name, the Children's Home at Easton. It moved into a bigger building on North Street, right near the Episcopal Church.

No doubt the hundreds of children who spent time there had varied experiences, from happy to unhappy and from productive to pointless. No social scientists tracked the life outcomes of its residents. My research turned up snippets from the lives of three "friendless" orphans.

First, though, I should probably share a touching reminder of the home's mission from a *Baltimore Sun* article in 1925:

Every little life in the shelter of the home is linked with a story of death, despair, and desolation.

"Dearest boy" George Todd is an oddity in the history of the orphanage. He snuck into the Home for Friendless Children on day one, just in time. Very soon after that the orphanage powers that be decided it would be a girls-only facility. George soon found himself sharing living quarters with 13 girls. The girls lived dormitory style, with old photos showing six, eight, or more small beds laid out in big rooms. George, on the other hand, lived like Harry Potter in the dreary Dursley period of his youth. Instead of a cupboard under the stairs, it was a "cubby hole" under the eaves.

The distaff-thick environment didn't stop George from embracing traditional gender roles. He loved anything that positioned him as the "man of the house"—manual labor, farm chores, all of it.

That barn, how he loved it! It was his castle, and the cow, the cat and her kittens, the chickens, and the one pig were his subjects.

When the situation called for it, George was a good sport about girlish things. Even though "nothing sissy held his attention too long," he would agree on rainy days to "play house" with the girls. He stayed at the Home for Friendless Children for three years. Then the home placed him with a local family. His going away party involved lots of singing and praying.

Soft notes emanated from the organ. George, now 11, sang with his head thrown back, shoulders squared, letting the notes roll.

George Todd grew up to become a plumber. He was living in Oxford when he passed away in the 1950s. He must have been about 80.

Norma Higgins arrived at the orphanage very late in the game, in 1953, after the death of her father. She was 13 then. She was 78 when she shared recollections for a 2014 article in the *Star Democrat* newspaper.

Norma regarded her adolescence as "typical." Her daily routine involved waking up early and tackling chores before heading off to school, "like any other teenager." She had a curfew. She attended school dances. She and her housemates got Christmas gifts, suitable clothes, and other things through the generosity of "sponsors." Often, those sponsors were local families who "adopted" a child. Civic groups and churches pitched in on the "adoption" front as well. The home had started in 1871 with one adult staffer. Now it had four, but they were still operating in accord with the home's founding principles.

They were like mothers to us. They cared about us, and they loved us. If we had any problems we would sit and talk to them, and they would help us in any way they could. I really enjoyed everything about living there.

She and the other girls had a fun nickname for themselves:

Poor little rich girls.

Norma never felt stigma about her orphanage-girl status. She didn't remember school classmates from intact families looking down on her or making mean comments. She spent five years at the home, leaving at age 18 to marry her high school sweetheart, Richard Higgins.

She and Richard made their home in the watermen community of Neavitt along the backroads of Talbot County. They ran a seafood business and a hunting guide service. They had three children. Norma died in 2023. Her obituary doesn't mention the Children's Home. It focuses at first on her professional accomplishments, detailing the many key roles she played in the family businesses. Later, there is this:

She was the backbone of her family and in all their endeavors nothing was more important to her than her children feeling secure in a loving home. She enjoyed cooking and baking and was happiest when hosting holiday and special occasion feasts for family and friends. Her biscuits are legend in Talbot County.

Friendless No More: Polly
Youth is versatile, turning easily from one type of life to another.

The third orphan here both lived in and wrote about the home. Polly Pobst arrived at age nine, in 1925. Her mother had died of tuberculosis, leaving her blacksmith father to care for six children. He tried his best to keep the family together, hiring one "housekeeper" after another. But none of them stuck for long in their Galestown home.

The last woman in that run of caretakers brought her own two daughters into the house. The new girls and the Pobst kids didn't get along. One fracas ended with one of the new girls hurling a lamp at Polly. When Polly and her dad got back from getting Polly stitched up at the hospital, the woman and her girls were gone.

That's when Mr. Pobst gave up, placing his two daughters in the Children's Home. It's unclear what happened to his four boys, though at least some of them stayed with their father. Polly arrived in the same year the Baltimore *Sun* reported that the home was barely getting by "on a meager income, sometimes scarcely knowing where the next funds would come from."

Polly never saw any hints of those financial woes. *Unto the Least of These*—the book she wrote later in life (under a married name, Polly Ross)—is a mix of personal memoir and affectionate institutional history. Several of the anecdotes above about the founding of the home come from her work.

Ross's book is chock full of charming, old-style writing. Here she is, recalling the day of her arrival:

Sunlight glinted on the dew-drenched ivy creeping up the stuccoed walls [and] forming a lovely pattern like silver beads crocheted. There was nothing forbidding about the home. Indeed it seemed peaceful and serene, its wings stretched out on both sides as though to welcome little children in need of a home.

A staffer led Polly, her sister, and her father on a tour. Polly got in trouble when she started climbing a tree. A staffer admonished her to get back down, pronto.

We can't have the neighbors thinking we are raising tomboys here.

Polly and her sister were dumbstruck at the sight of the children's playroom. Neither had ever owned so much as a doll. She settled into her new life quickly. Early on, a socialite named Mrs. Skillen took a liking to Polly and offered to adopt her. Polly had mixed feelings. Her father ended up making that decision.

Tell the lady that though I appreciate her offer I don't want my girls separated. I'd like them to grow up together.

Mrs. Skillen took the rejection well. She became Polly's informal "godmother," taking her on boat rides and shopping trips and picnic excursions. They often sipped tea together at Riley's Tea Shop. They shared frequent lunches at the Hotel Avon.

Visiting day at the home fell on the first Sunday of each month. Polly's father (who had moved to Federalsburg by this point) called on his girls on most of those days, though sometimes his ramshackle Model T didn't cooperate. One such Sunday found Polly waiting in a room with other girls, all hoping their names would be called because they had a visitor.

Polly's heart jumped with joy when she heard her name. But then another girl in the room broke into tears. Polly tried to console her. The girl made a heartbreaking confession.

I pray so hard for someone to come to see me, but God does not hear me. I think he must be looking the other way whenever I pray.

The girl told Polly she'd been praying like that every visiting day for *six years*. Polly told her father this story, and he knew just what to do. Instead of seeing only his two girls on visitation Sundays, he would see four girls—the two others being a rotating cast of girls who rarely or never got visitors.

Dad was a true gentleman and understood their predicament. He did not ask embarrassing questions but talked of things in general. He told them of his work, how as a boy he had a genuine love for horses and how now it was a real pleasure to outfit them with new shoes. They hung on his words with rapt, attentive faces. They listened, paying no attention to his poor humped back

218

bent from many hours of lowly labor. Indeed all they saw was a man, a big-hearted man who had cared enough to share his visit to his daughters with them. He had not given us money or gifts. He could not afford to do that. But he had given us something a whole lot more precious, himself.

Like Norma Higgins, Polly Pobst looked back on her childhood as blessedly normal. Girls at the home didn't miss out on civic activities. They went to movies, concerts, circuses, carnivals, and lectures. They went on vacations too, once for a full week in New York City. (Be sure to read the afternote at the end here—it's a sweet story about summertime trips the orphan girls took to Ocean City, Md.)

Sometimes I felt we were the most fortunate children in the whole world.

She stayed at the home nearly 10 years, departing after graduating from high school. She landed in the home of a local family named Mills, working as a servant, basically, in exchange for room and board. She scrubbed floors, washed windows, darned socks, and cared for children.

She lost her way in life during this transition. Her confidence faltered. Feeling inadequate in these new surroundings she stayed to herself and mostly avoided interacting with the rest of the family. She found herself in church one Sunday, the service over. Polly was by herself, sitting in a pew, when she overheard a woman nearby ask a friend:

Who is that child over there, the one that sits with the Mills?

219

The reply:

*Oh she's their servant, taken from the children's home. ... I under-
stand she is quite dull, seldom ever talks, never laughs. But then
you know how children are who have been raised on charity.*

That insult proved to be the kick in the pants Polly needed. It got
her to thinking about all the skills she had learned at the home,
all the literature she'd read, all the artwork she'd studied, all the
friends she'd made, and all the adventures she'd had. What did
she have to feel ashamed about? She soon got over that inferiority
complex and got back to tackling life with a little more gusto.

*I often think of and pray for that Lady who referred to me as the
child raised on charity. I can now lift my head high and say, "Yes,
I was brought up in the children's home on charity. On REAL
Christian charity."*

Polly would eventually earn a degree from Chesapeake College.
She worked as a dental nurse in addition to writing two books and
numerous articles for various publications. She died in Easton in
2017 at the age of 91.

Afternote #1: The Orphan Girls in Ocean City
We've already seen that orphans at the Home for Friendless Children actually had lots of friends—sponsors, donors, etc. In her
book *Unto the Least of These*, Polly Ross devotes a few pages to
an extra special friend, Edgar Ijams.

Think about July in Ocean City, Md. Whether today or in
the 1920s doesn't matter. Either way, you wouldn't expect a hotel
there to be giving away free rooms in peak tourism season. Espe-

cially not a prime hotel like the Plimhimmon, which ranked as the pinnacle of Ocean City hospitality in the 1920s.

Casino, concert hall, renowned restaurant, elegant rooms with newfangled electricity. If you look at old photos of Ocean City, the Plimhimmon is the building that will make you go weak at the knees and long to travel back in time. Oh, those wrap-around porches! That glorious dome atop the roof!

Every July in the late 1920s hotel manager Edgar Ijams invited 40 or so orphan girls from Easton to be his guests.

We were never treated as orphans, but as paying patrons.

Every morning Mr. Ijams would join the girls for breakfast. He often invited VIPs to those meals—prominent guests, civic leaders, business colleagues, and the like. The girls had to earn their breakfast by singing to Mr. Ijams and his guests.

Word got out around town about the orphan girls and their singing. They were easily identified, all dressed identically in "bloomers and mini blouses." When the girls walked down the boardwalk, shop owners and restaurant managers would call out to them, promising to "treat" the girls if they would sing a song.

We sang for saltwater taffy, popcorn, rides on the merry go round, and even the rented bathing suits.

The trips were an annual ritual during Polly's time at the home. Here is how she concludes her memories of those vacations:

How refreshing it was to be so close to God, sitting there early in the morning filling my little girl's heart and soul with the beauty of Ocean City, Maryland.

It's pretty clear in context that she wasn't referring just to the natural wonders of the sun coming up over the beach, but also to the beauty inside the hearts of the generous people of Ocean City.

Afternote #2: Still Going

Why did the Children's Home shut down in 1958? Basically, because times change. Orphanages fell out of fashion over the years, replaced by a focus on foster care. After the home shut down, the charitable organization behind it kept right on running—and it's still doing good works today. The Children's Home Foundation of the Eastern Shore provides financial aid to students with a focus on developing job skills that will last a lifetime. They also give away scholarships to summer camp programs.

27 RESILIENCE
THE MUSHROOM LADY OF TALBOT COUNTY BLAZES A TRAIL

How do you feel about mushrooms? Not on pizza or with pasta, but in the forest, growing wild. Most people barely notice them during hikes, focusing instead on flowers and trees and birds. What if I told you about a woman from days gone by who went hiking all the time, but focused nearly all her sensory energy on fungi? Day in, day out. Year after year. Decade after decade. You might ask:

Was she crazy?

So let's start there. It's the 1890s. Imagine you're riding what passed then for a bus—a big, open, horse-drawn carriage clattering along a city street. The vehicle is jam-packed. A woman squeezes aboard. She's about 70, a little on the stout side. Folks who knew her said her demeanor was "pleasant, but somewhat erratic." So maybe imagine a twitch, a tick, talking to herself, or some other oddity.

223

It's quite possible that her clothes were streaked with dirt. She carries a basket loaded to the brim with mud and mushrooms. That's why, all of a sudden, the carriage stinks to high heaven. The scientific name for the variety of mushroom in that basket is *phallus duplicatus*, or "netted stinkhorn." It's one of the world's foulest smelling fungi, with an odor that lands somewhere between rotten meat and a pile of steaming dog poo.

The kicker: Flies go insane for netted stinkhorn. Suddenly, the windowless carriage is swarming with a Biblical-level plague of overstimulated insects. Even the mushroom lady herself would find this particular ride memorable.

The smell had increased to such an extent that the flies nearly devoured me, in their eagerness to get at the fungus.

The mushroom lady got lucky. None of her fellow travelers flew into a rage. No one grabbed her bucket and tossed it overboard. The other passengers just sucked it up, sitting in "stony silence for the duration of the trip." But you know that when they got home, they regaled their families with a nightmarish tale of the crazy lady and her foul-smelling mushrooms.

It's a shame those people didn't know that the story they told had so many other twists and turns, plus a surprise ending to boot. Through a mix of persistence, pluck, and smarts, that crazy mushroom lady beat long odds in life. At a time when the world regarded the notion of women in science as ridiculous, Mary Banning ranked among the top mushroom-studying mycologists of her day, even if no one would realize what she had accomplished until nearly a century after she died.

'Toadstools Have Claimed My Imagination'

Mary Banning's fascination with fungi began in rural Talbot County, on Maryland's Eastern Shore. Born in 1822 she grew up on Hopkins Neck, a peninsula between the towns of St. Michaels and Easton. The Bannings were (and still are) a prominent family in the area. Mary's grandfather served as a delegate at the meeting where Maryland ratified the U.S. Constitution. Her father served in the state legislature.

Hopkins Neck had a glorious view of the mouth of Plain-dealing Creek, but in childhood Mary was drawn less to water and more to woods. Along the trails near her home she swooned over the "mystery," the "beauty," and the intricate architectural "structure" of mushrooms.

From early childhood, toadstools have claimed my imagination.

Girls weren't supposed to dream of futures in the botanical sciences back then. Mary's parents didn't have the option of enrolling their daughter in a STEM program at school. Heck, there weren't any public schools when Mary was a child.

She was a young adult when her fungi fascination shifted into overdrive. The turning point was a charity project for a "mission school." It's unclear in the historical record which school this was, but she seems to have wanted to serve some group or another of underprivileged children. She wanted to teach those kids to appreciate nature. When the notion of focusing on mushrooms popped into her head, she at first laughed it off as ridiculous.

Have you ever had an idea that grabbed hold of your mind and wouldn't let go? The mushroom curriculum idea kept circling back to the front of her mind.

With few exceptions, fungi are considered botanic outcasts. Like beggars by the wayside dressed in gay attire, they ask for attention but claim none.

Was it really a silly idea, showing children the way God's glories shine even in the most disrespected of living things? Banning surrendered to the mushroom curriculum concept, regarding it as a perfect "means of teaching faith" and "of cultivating minds and morals."

I didn't find any reports about academic outcomes for those kids, but this was the shift in thinking that marked the start of Mary's transition from casual nature lover to obsessive mushroom hunter. She adopted a regular practice of venturing into woods, collecting specimens and writing up descriptions. She took up a brush and started painting lush, intricate watercolors of the various species. She visited libraries, poring through documents about the science of mycology.

'Poor thing. ... Clean gone mad!'

She encountered her share of challenges along the way. She was in her mid-20s when her father died. His survivors fell on somewhat hard times after that. She moved to Baltimore in the 1850s with her mother and a sister. Both had health issues, and Mary was their primary caretaker.

She seems to have had enough money to get by, living modestly. Even with those caretaker duties, she still carved out windows for mushroom hunting and studying. She would run off into forestlands whenever she could—not just around Baltimore, but up in Pennsylvania, over in Virginia, and elsewhere in the Mid-Atlantic region.

When arriving in unfamiliar territory, she sometimes

asked locals for advice. She knew just which type of people to ask, judging by the story of one trip during which she approached a trio of "very bright" looking young boys on the street, asking if they knew where mushrooms grew in abundance nearby. They responded with enthusiasm, and Banning "engaged them to come to the hotel the next morning and conduct me to, as they called it, 'a grand place for frog stools.'"

The boys were so excited by the prospect of this mushroom-hunting adventure that they couldn't wait. They went into the forest early the next morning, without Banning, and then showed up at the hotel, clothes and faces probably streaked with mud. One boy had a load of mushrooms in his hat. Another had a bucket and the third had a basket, both overflowing with fungi. They approached the maître d'.

We want to see the frog-stool lady that stays here.

That maître d' did what any self-respecting maître d' would do under such circumstances. He screamed at the boys.

You scamps clear out this moment! Off with you! Have you gone crazy? Whoever heard of a frog-stool lady?!

In a stroke of luck Mary Banning was standing in the lobby at that moment, close enough to overhear the ruckus. She walked up. One boy cried out:

There she be!

Another boy:

Didn't I tell you so?

Mary Banning knew full well that lots of people thought of her vocation the way that maître d' did, as unthinkable, especially for a woman, and perhaps even insane. The gentler skeptics regarded her as "just a little Quixotic," but others rendered harsher judgments. One day a man who knew about Mary's mushroom-hunting habit asked in passing if she had found any "frog stools" on that day's outing. Alas, she had not.

And it's a blessed thing you can't find 'em!...Pison [sic] things... Better let frog stools alone! That's my advice to everyone.

The man walked away, muttering:

Poor thing. Crazy, certain sure. Clean gone mad!

Mary endured many moments like this, but she learned to get over the hurt. Eventually, she came to regard the skeptics with a mix of stubborn pride and thoughtful generosity.

Both in Maryland and Virginia I get no help in the way of finding plants. The idea of looking for 'frogstools' is burlesqued.... There is no sympathy for the work. In fact they regard it as ridiculous. All this has not the slightest effect upon me, save in retarding my progress in the work. I hire a carriage, wagon, or any sort of vehicle I can get, start off to do good work, but they regard me as a crazy woman, fit to be placed in a straitjacket. Is it not laughable! How I do pity their ignorance.

'I Took the Duty that God Placed Before Me'
There were, however, a few times in life when Mary Banning felt
sorry for herself. She wondered how much more she might have
accomplished as a mycologist if those family caretaking duties
hadn't occupied so much time. But here, too, she found her way
accepting the turns of a complex life, brushing off any festering
regrets.

*I am never too sick to take up an interest in fungi and flowers. I
wish I had given my whole life up to that study. I believe I should
now be an expert in every department, but home duties occupied
my time in early days and perhaps I am not right in feeling a
regret. I had rather die with the feeling of having done my duty
than die with the feeling of having gratified an undying love for
botany. Both were before me, but I took [on] the duty that God
placed before me. I think I have been right.*

Friends and relatives spoke of Mary's "high ideals, her charity,
and always of her delight in nature." In addition to mushroom
hunting, she loved to press flowers. On the tablecloths, bed linens,
and towels in her house were little "sketches" done in "indelible
ink" of animals she saw and studied on her woodland adventures.
Another curious little hobby: She would dissect fish, then tie their
bones back up with wire and put the bodies back together.

By the late 1880s age was catching up with Mary Banning. Both her mother and sister had died. She was battling
multiple chronic illnesses. She was losing her eyesight. She had
not worked to this point in complete anonymity. She had corresponded with professional male mycologists, asking for advice
and sharing discoveries. She had published a few small essays in
scientific publications, including *The Botanical Gazette* and the

Bulletin of the Torrey Botanical Club.

But her dream was much bigger: She had assembled a book manuscript based on her 20-plus years of botanical study and mushroom hunting, containing watercolors and scientific descriptions of 175 varieties.

Looking back from the perspective of today, that manuscript was an extraordinary accomplishment. Up to that time a grand total of one book had been published dedicated to the science of American mushrooms. More remarkable: Banning's book featured 23 species previously unknown to science. And then there were those incredible watercolors, a sublime mix of scientific illustration and outsider folk art.

Modern-day historians of science agree: The "crazy" lady swarmed by flies on that carriage bus ranked among the best mycologists in the Mid-Atlantic region, perhaps even among the best in the country.

'Each a Glory Bright'
Mary Banning didn't have the money or the connections to get that book published. So she faced a big question in her older years: What to do with the culminating triumph of her 20-plus years of botanical study?

One of the scientists she had traded letters with was Charles Peck of the New York State Museum. He was a big deal, on his way to a prominence that would have later historians bestow upon him the title of "dean of American mycologists," and he seems to have corresponded with Banning in a way that earned her trust.

So in 1890 Mary Banning packed up her manuscript and mailed it to Peck. Perhaps the dean of American mycologists was busy that day, too engrossed in some deadline to give a serious look to Mary Banning's opus. He put the manuscript aside.

He never got back to it. It ended up in some random stack of old documents or another, and at some point that stack landed in storage, lost and unfiled. No one looked at it for a month, six months, a year, a decade.

Ninety-one years.

Mary Banning died on Feb. 28, 1903. On the surface her departure from the world seems a sad affair. She lived her last days in a convalescent boarding house in Winchester, Va. As the end approached she requested that no one be given written notice of her death. She asked that nothing be published about her passing in newspapers back in Maryland. And this:

I wish no invitations given to my funeral except to my old nurse Dolly Denny (colored), and to Clementina Gladden (colored).

But wait. Here, I am feeling a personal need to interject with a note of caution against assuming the worst about Banning's last days. I have seen in my own family how frail, ailing, elderly loved ones can form deep and magical bonds with caretakers. Who knows? Perhaps Dolly and Clementina were the best friends Mary Banning ever had.

Mary left the little money she still had to an orphanage. She had her books and other possessions sent to a relative in Delaware.

And no one heard a peep about her life and accomplishments until 1981. That's when a mycologist named John Haynes stumbled upon Banning's manuscript while rooting through archives at the New York State Museum. He was blown away. He sensed straight away that he had stumbled upon an important document in the history of American mycology. More than that:

an important chapter in the history of women in science.

Haynes organized a special exhibit at the New York State Museum devoted to Mary Banning and her work. That show was such a success that it went on the road, appearing at several other universities and science museums. Haynes also wrote up a mini-biography of Banning that was published in *Maryland Naturalist.*

That's why, if you go searching on the internet today, you will find that Mary Banning has won at long last a good measure of the renown she so richly deserves, both as a mycologist and as a woman of science. She's in the Maryland Women's Hall of Fame. She has a mushroom named in her honor, the *Amanita banningiana*, or the Mary Banning Splendid Caesar, although as of this writing that name has still not achieved official "published" status in the scientific community.

Let's imagine for a second that Mary Banning was able to look down from heaven and watch as her life's work emerged out into the world at last. I suspect that she might have taken special pride in the title of that traveling exhibit:

Each a Glory Bright

That's where Mary Banning started, remember? By thinking about how wonderful it is that God's glory is reflected even in "botanic outcasts," "beggars by the wayside." The title gets at another, larger truth, this one touching on all the people who regarded her as crazy for stepping outside the bounds of social mores to live the life of a lady mushroom hunter. The next time we jump to the overly quick conclusion that some random stranger must be crazy—hey, give a thought to Mary Banning and remember: "Each a Glory Bright."

28 INTERLUDE
THE SNOW SHOVELING
BRIGADE OF OCEAN CITY, 1922

A blizzard in February of 1922 left Ocean City blanketed in snow. The roads were impassible, to cars and carriages alike. There were no snow plows coming—that government service was still way off in the future. In ordinary circumstances, this would be no problem. Folks were used to it. They'd wait for the snow to melt and then get on with life.

But circumstances were not ordinary. When the snow stopped falling, folks who lived near the oceanfront discovered a "great monster of the sea" sprawled on the beach. The dead whale was nearly 60 feet long.

Kids walked to school in those days. Edgar Gaskins plodded through the snow for two miles to get to class. When he arrived, the whole school was abuzz with news of the sea monster. Those kids trudged home and told their parents and neighbors. Everybody in the area wanted to go see the behemoth.

Gaskins recounted this episode in his memoir, *Yesteryears: A Bit of Ocean City History & Heritage*. He claims that the people of Ocean City responded to the challenge at hand by launching "the most unique" snow removal project ever "put into operation, before or since."

That might be a bit of an overstatement. But still, it was an impressive display of can-do community cooperation.

[Soon] every Model T Ford truck available in the countryside was loaded with neighbors, each with a shovel. The line of trucks moved slowly along the snow-covered road, stopping when the snow in front of the first truck made going on impossible. Every man, boy, and child around, with a shovel, helped out and opened the road. The cars moved forward inch by inch. The stopping and digging continued until the beach was reached and the whale admired.

Afternote
What happened to the whale? Now that's a fun story, too—it's up on the Secrets of the Eastern Shore website. Search there for the word *whale.* Spoilers:

It became a giant tourist attraction, causing traffic jams. It started to smell. They towed it out to sea. It floated back in. They carved it up into big chunks and dropped those chunks in various ocean locations. A big chunk floated back in. It really smelled now. They dynamited it. Some folks claim that the aroma of dead whale lingered around the boardwalk for years afterward.

29 RESILIENCE
THE SURVIVOR: ROBERT BANKS AND THE PRICE OF FREEDOM

Imagine a young soldier stationed halfway around the world. He's been through hell on the battlefield and landed in a prison camp where food comes in starvation rations, infectious diseases run rampant, and winter nights descend in a bone-chilling freeze deeper than anything he's ever known. His comrades in arms are dropping like flies, their bodies tossed unceremoniously into ditches.

One thing keeps this young man going—a faith planted deep inside of his heart by a beloved mother and a devout church community back home on the Eastern Shore of Maryland. He dreams time and again of his mother's hot biscuits and cornpone. He thinks often of how she probably doesn't even know whether he's dead or alive.

Then comes a day when his captors toss him a bone. They give him permission to write a letter home and tell his mother that he's still alive, still holding onto the faith she imbued in his heart. Robert Banks turned that offer down.

As we'll see, he made that decision with a heart full of love.

235

The First 17 Years: From Cambridge to Japan

First, some background. Banks was 17 years old when he joined the Army on Jan. 14, 1948. The son of William and Lillie Banks, he'd grown up in working-class fashion in Cambridge, Md. Newspapers of the time describe his father as a laborer and his mother as a "semi-invalid." The family home on bustling Washington Street stood a few short blocks from Bethel AME Church—that historic house of worship was a centerpiece of Banks's childhood years.

After basic training in Texas, Banks landed in Japan with the 24th Infantry Regiment. That unit has a place in the history books—it was the last all-black force in a U.S. military that was slowly but surely desegregating in the post-World War II years. Banks was probably stationed at Camp Gifu, the focal point of the 24th's peacekeeping work. Located 250 miles west of Tokyo Gifu ranked as a remote, low-key, and uneventful outpost—just the sort of assignment military authorities preferred back then for all-black units.

By all accounts the 24th had it pretty good in Gifu. They were mostly left alone by white higher-ups, some of whom had well-documented histories of meddling unfairly in the affairs of black units. The camp boasted amenities quite lavish by the standards of the time. The USO put on frequent shows at the Easly Theater. The Red Cross installed a lounge, a game room, a library, and a patio. In a book about the 24th Infantry during these years, historians William T. Bowers, William M. Hammond, and George L. MacGarrigle point out that many soldiers had come from impoverished backgrounds.

Overall, life with the regiment was so pleasant that it exceeded anything many of the soldiers had ever known.

That peaceful time in Gifu came to an abrupt end in the summer of 1950 when tensions on the nearby Korean Peninsula erupted into civil war. The United Nations sent troops—mostly American—to support a beleaguered South Korean army.

The 24th got its orders to join the fight early in that war. The transition out of Gifu was a rocky affair. Many soldiers reacted with anger when commanders denied them permission to go into town one last time. Quite a few of those soldiers counted local Japanese women as girlfriends. Some had been in Gifu long enough to have children and form makeshift families. A bunch of soldiers slipped out of camp in defiance of that stay-out-of-town order. Things got raucous that night—the incident became the subject of an official Army inquiry.

Captured on the Banks of the Yalu
The Korean War unfolded in three big waves. The war began with a surprise North Korean attack that very nearly won the war, pushing South Korean and U.N. forces to the brink of defeat. But the allies held on at a last-ditch refuge in the city of Busan. Fresh troops and supplies soon arrived through that city's port, putting the allies in position to counterattack.

The offensive that followed nearly won the war in turn, with the allies advancing deep into what is now North Korean territory. In November 1950 Robert Banks and his comrades in the 24th were in the vanguard of that push. Banks did his part along the way—and then some. He won a Bronze Medal for combat heroics, though it hadn't yet been officially pinned on his chest. He earned a promotion to sergeant, though the paperwork hadn't yet gone through.

The war's third wave began with an unexpected and horrible surprise. The 24th was operating quite close to the border with China along the Yalu River when Chinese troops entered the war, surging across the Yalu in an overwhelming show of force. Banks got caught in the middle of that surprise.

Millions and millions of Chinese came running at us. We were surrounded. I was captured.

That short quotation from an old newspaper article barely hints at the horrors that unfolded on the battlefield. Banks's daughter, LaShon Foster, says that her father and a good number of his colleagues tried to evade capture by laying amid "stacks of dead bodies," some already decomposing. While trying to stay still and feign death, those soldiers could feel rats and mice nibbling on their limbs.

That third wave saw Chinese and North Korean forces push the allies back toward South Korea. The fighting would end in a tense stalemate at the "38th Parallel," which still serves today as the border between the two Koreas.

Banks missed out on all but the start of that third-wave action. He had written home every week without fail during his time overseas, but the letters stopped arriving back in Cambridge after one dated Nov. 23, 1950. His name first appeared on an official missing-in-action report on Dec. 28, 1950. He had three years in the service at this point—he was 20 years old.

Desperate Days in 'Camp Five'
Banks would spend most of the next three years on the banks of the Yalu, enduring life in the most notorious and deadly of North Korean prison camps. POWs in "Camp Five" slept on dirt floors in mud huts. Their diet for long periods consisted almost entirely

of "cracked corn." A piece of bread might show up on rare occasions.

The winter months of early 1951 were brutally cold, even by North Korean standards. Those huts had no reliable sources of heat. The prisoners had no lamps or candles. They were given no coats or other scraps of winter clothing.

If North Korean guards decided that a POW had been "disobedient"—and they often did so for trivial transgressions—they often put the offender in "The Ice Box" That's what POWs called a vault that had survived the bombing of a bank building. Quite a few prisoners died from the cold in that box.

Banks's daughter LaShon Foster learned from her father about another brand of torture that is not mentioned in old newspaper interviews. Prisoners were lined up and told to stand on one leg, balancing as if in a yoga tree pose. If they let their airborne foot touch the ground, they were sometimes shot in the head. Foster says that on at least one occasion her father held his pose while the men on either side of him were murdered.

In later newspaper accounts, reporters quoted Banks using two main words to describe his early months of captivity. The first was *brutality*, for obvious reasons, but the second was *monotony*. Many days passed in endless and empty fashion, broken up only by re-education sessions filled with anti-American propaganda. No exercise periods, no books, no organized activities.

Robert Banks guesstimated in later interviews that 30 to 40 prisoners died every day early on in his stay at Camp Five. The U.S. Department of Defense puts the death toll among POWs held in all the North Korean camps at 7,614. The most common cause was infectious disease (66%), aggravated by the complete absence of quality medical care. The second-leading cause of death was "external causes" (11%), a category that covers a broad range of violence, ranging from the torture and murder of prisoners to fatalities caused by errant bombing strikes or gunfire from nearby battles that sprayed into the camp. Here is what Banks would say years later about the suffering he witnessed:

As long as I live I will remember those buddies, between five and six hundred, some of whom wandered around the prison camp, crazed [and] untended until some got so bad they had to take them away. ... The men dying like flies, and the POWs digging trenches in the bleak ground around the hills along the Yalu. And the broken bodies going into the shallow trench, with no one to say a word.

He tried his best to do some small measure of spiritual justice by the lost souls:

I prayed, as my mother taught me, silently, that the good Lord would take care of them at home in heaven.

Banks's son, also named Robert, says his father later told the family how he would sometimes look around at his fellow prisoners, wondering which of them would dig the trench that his own body would land in when the time came.

This is why Robert Banks Sr. decided against writing a letter home to his mother when that opportunity arose. He figured he was probably going to end up in one of those ditches. Why give a beloved mother hope, when that hope was almost sure to be dashed?

It's unclear how many months these darkest of days lasted, but Camp Five eventually underwent a transition for the better. More professional Chinese soldiers took over from the

North Koreans. The food got a little more plentiful. POWs were allowed to stoke underground fires and warm up those mud huts on cold nights. They had fuel-oil lamps. They could play a little soccer and football. They sometimes were allowed to go swimming in a restricted area of the Yalu.

Banks began to regain a measure of physical strength. More importantly, his spiritual state improved, especially after those Chinese guards began allowing men Banks described as the "better educated" POWs to lead Bible readings and hold makeshift religious services.

The longing for home got us down at times, [but] then we would "spread the Good Word" [among each other, that] God is here just the same as at home, and someday we'll go home.

It was during these days of rejuvenation—the spring of 1952—that Banks changed his mind and began writing letters home. His first missive was a Mother's Day greeting.

Much later, in the early 1970s, a newspaper reporter would interview Banks and two other former Korean POWs about their experiences. The idea behind the story was to help local families who at that time were welcoming POWs home from Vietnam. All three Korean War veterans warned that letters home from prison camps "painted rosy pictures" that did not reflect the horrors they were enduring.

One example: Banks sent a photo to his mother during this period showing him diving happily into the Yalu River. Here is LaShon Foster:

My dad told us that what you did not see in that picture was the guns drawn on him and his fellow prisoners, forcing them to pre-

241

tend they were being treated right.

Homecoming for a Hero
Back on Washington Street in Cambridge, the long wait had start-ed with that first official missing-in-action report from December of 1950. Lillie Banks passed a full year not knowing whether her son was dead or alive. Then, in December 1951, the name Robert Banks appeared on North Korea's list of captured soldiers. Here is what Lillie said to a newspaper reporter that day:

I always had a feeling he was still alive. We prayed day and night for him. It's all I want for Christmas. It means everything that [my son is] alive.

Seventeen more months passed without word. Then, at last, that Mother's Day missive arrived in May 1952. More letters rolled in after that.

The war drew to a close. Banks was released after two years, eight months, and 13 days in Camp Five. The Army sent him and thousands of other newly freed prisoners home by way of slow-moving ship rather than high-flying plane. The extra time allowed for physical exams, mental health evaluations, and depro-gramming of brainwash victims.

Banks was now 23 years old. Upon meeting him in per-son, one reporter described Banks as "physically frail but spiritu-ally strong." He had lost nearly 40 pounds.

[But] he knows his mother ... will take care of that with good home cooking.

A ship carrying Banks and 327 other POWs arrived in San Francisco in August 1953. Some of the POWs aboard were from the West Coast—their families came out to welcome them home. From a newspaper account of that day:

On the pier below, many a wife sighted her husband and many a mother her son and started a happy shout—only to find that it came out a sob. Some children, bewildered because they didn't quite understand it all, huddled in their mothers' arms, their backs to the fathers they had never seen or could barely remember. Flash bulbs popped and broadcasters dashed to and fro, dragging tangles of cable. But neither the repatriates nor their families minded.

Robert Banks probably watched that reunion scene, but he had to wait for his own reunion moment. His plane landed at Friendship Airport (now Baltimore Washington International Airport) on Aug. 24. From there he went to the Baltimore home of a relative.

I was talking to a reporter [outside] when my mother first sighted me as she came down the street. She screamed. I heard her and turned. I ran to her. She kissed and hugged me and said in a choked voice, "Son, we're proud to have you back." I could only say, ... "I'm proud to be back."

The City of Cambridge pulled out all the stops to welcome Banks back to the Eastern Shore. City officials and American Legion leaders met Banks's car just outside of town, then led the hero of the hour through town in a 40-car motorcade that crawled along behind two drum-and-bugle corps.

Almost the entire population of Cambridge lined the flag-decorat-

ed streets as the parade honoring the 23-year-old Negro veteran traveled to the Municipal Building. The crowds were especially thick in the Second Ward, [the historically African-American neighborhood where the Banks family lived].

When the motorcade stopped at City Hall, Mayor Russell P. Smith had this to say:

It is with pleasure that I welcome you back, not only to your mother and father, friends and relatives, but to the city of Cambridge. A mother's prayers are answered. You are a symbol to all those people who lost their boys. You are a shining example of courage and determination to help your country and all those of the free world who fought and suffered for justice. I salute you.

Gifts were given. Commendations were awarded. During a ceremony at American Legion Post 87 Lillie Banks was presented with a corsage and asked to say a few words.

I am so happy at having my son back that I can't say any more. I am thankful from the bottom of my heart.

Then Robert Banks himself was called up. He managed a total of five words:

I'm proud to be back.

In the days that followed there were many interviews with various newspapers. One of those contained a quote from Robert Banks that seems a fitting way to close out the chapter of his ordeal that ended with this homecoming celebration.

It was my mother's faith, her teachings right here [in Cambridge] when I was a boy, to believe in God and our way of life, that kept me sane and free in mind all those dreary days.

The Price Paid by Robert Banks

I wish that I could report that the war ended for Robert Banks at that point, but it didn't. He spent many months at a military hospital in Pennsylvania, receiving care for an old bullet wound and myriad other physical problems. Doctors decided that removing that bullet ran too high a risk of paralysis, so it remained lodged in his spine for the rest of his days.

Banks went to school to become an electrician. In Cambridge he opened his own business, repairing TVs and doing electrical work. He also worked in a local factory owned by National Can. He sometimes took on extra part-time jobs.

Banks married Guinervere Cornish in 1956. They would have seven children together, two of whom shared details with me by email about the struggles their father endured in his postwar life. Make no mistake, however, about the most important thing those children want you to know about their father. LaShon Foster:

My father was the greatest father of all time. The children of Robert I. Banks would never trade him for billions. He was one of the kindest men we have ever known, and if people go to heaven now, my father is sitting there.

Robert Banks's ordeal never ended. In addition to physical problems he struggled mightily with post-traumatic stress disorder. His mind would sometimes drift back into the war zone. He struggled with alcohol addiction. This potent mix could knock

245

him off mental balance and set him off in uncontrollable rages. LaShon Foster:

When daddy would go back into time and think that he was on the battlefield, his children suddenly became the enemy.

His children had to flee the family home during these episodes. Their safe spot was the home of their grandmother—the same woman whose teachings and faith Robert Banks credited for his ability to survive everything he endured in Camp Five. As the oldest child, Robert Jr. tried his best to protect his siblings. He would create a diversion, distracting his father and taking the brunt of his fury so that his siblings had time to reach a designated safe spot. LaShon Foster:

We called my grandmother's house "home base." Once you arrived there, you were protected. He could not cross that door in one of his rages, no matter how crazed he was from his nightmares and PTSD.

Then the rage would pass. Foster continues:

The day after one of these attacks, he would buy you the world. There is nothing he would not do to make up for the night before. We don't know how many tears he cried. He hated every moment of his rages.

Once again: Those episodes and Banks's other struggles in life do not define the man in the memories of his children. When they recall Robert Banks, they think of his "heart of gold." Here is Robert Jr.:

We sometimes had little to spare, but my father would give to others from our pantry as if it was overstocked. He would feed the homeless and offer jobs to those who were overlooked in life. He would do TV-repair work based on a customer's promise to pay, then look the other way when they didn't pay.

LaShon Foster:

Our fondest memories are of a man who would give his life for you and me, a man who loved us unconditionally. And that is how we loved our father back, unconditionally—the good, the bad, and the ugly. He is our hero. He pushed us all. He wanted us not to be afraid, to stand tall for what we believed in.

Robert Banks died in 2008 at age 77. He suffered horribly at the end from liver and kidney failure, LaShon Foster says. In addition to his wife and children, Banks was survived at the time of his death by 19 grandchildren and 14 great-grandchildren.

One question is unavoidable here, considering all that Banks endured. If he had a chance to start over again, would he choose once more to sign up for the military at the tender age of 17? LaShon Foster says that every time that question came up her father replied in the same way.

He would quote the words from [country singer] Lee Greenwood: "I'm proud to be an American, where at least I know I'm free. I won't forget the men who died, who gave that right to me. Yes, I will gladly stand up and defend her still today. I love this land. God bless the USA."

Robert Banks Jr. sums up the story of his beloved father this way:

Only a few people ever heard the nightmare screams or watched him twist and turn and sweat the sheets wet. On many a night he would talk in his sleep about how they did this or that to him and his fellow prisoners. Guinervere Banks, his wife, always stood by his side as he fought the demons.

As his oldest son I often wonder how he ever made it through. Our father was small in size but a giant among men. He taught us that there's nothing you can't do if you give it your all and let God be your co-pilot through life. He loved life, even while carrying a tremendous amount of weight on his shoulders. He carried that weight all the way to the end. He was a survivor.

May Robert Banks rest in peace.

Afternote #1: Gratitude

My first version of this chapter was based entirely on old newspaper articles and other historical documents. It ended with a brief, just-the-facts summary of the postwar life of Robert Banks.

I shared that draft with family members, asking them to check it for mistakes. They caught a few, but then LaShon Foster and Robert Banks Jr. went beyond my request and shared the story of their father's postwar struggles and how those struggles impacted the family. Here is LaShon Foster explaining why they did that:

We want everyone to know that Robert Banks, our hero, came with a price. We want everyone to know that war affects many more people than just the soldier.

Afternote #2: Modern-Day Connections
The Banks family retains a strong presence in Cambridge today.

• Bank's daughter, LaShon Foster, has served in elective office as a city commissioner, been a candidate for mayor, and pitched in on many civic projects.

• Another of Banks's daughters, Janice Banks, became one of the first black women to join the volunteer Rescue Fire Company in Cambridge once that organization allowed blacks to join. She put in 30 years with RFC and remains an active member today.

• Banks's grand-nephew, Dion Banks, has also been involved in many civic projects, including one that would make Robert Banks proud—an effort to restore the building that houses Bethel AME Church to a fuller measure of its historical glory.

• Several of Robert Banks's descendants—including children, nieces, and nephews—have served our country in the military.

Afternote #3: The Japanese Connection
The 2008 obituary for Robert Banks notes that he was the father of one more child on top of the family he had with Guinervere. The list of surviving children includes "Roberta Banks of Honshu, Japan," which leads me to guess that Banks was among the members of the 24th who fathered children with Japanese girl-friends while stationed at Camp Gifu.

Afternote #4: An End to Military Segregation
Robert Banks entered Camp Five as a prisoner in November 1950. Eight months later, in July 1951, the Army announced plans

to disband his 24th Infantry Regiment as part of its slow-moving desegregation process. Fifteen months after that—in November 1952—the Army declared that desegregation project fully complete. Banks returned home from captivity in August of 1953.

Afternote #5: A Cautionary Note
For obvious reasons, people in Cambridge felt there was much to celebrate when Robert Banks returned home from captivity in 1953. They gave him a hero's welcome.

But Banks himself had mixed feelings about the festivities. Do you remember how he was interviewed in the 1970s by a reporter looking to offer advice to families and communities as they welcomed home prisoners of war from Vietnam? That reporter said that Banks and two fellow Korean POWs agreed on one tip.

[They] advised friends and families not to lavish too much attention on returning Vietnam prisoners and, for the first few months at least, not to ask too many questions.

Banks's son, Robert Jr., adds one more thing to consider here, and that surrounds the media coverage devoted to his father and his fellow POWs when they returned home. As Robert Banks and his family came to see things, Robert Jr. says, the only type of story reporters seemed interested in were "ones that benefited the press and showed how great this country was." The full story, as we have seen, can be much more complicated.

30 COURAGE
THE BRAVE MARCH OF THE BAREFOOT BOY

The best way to tell the inspiring story of how Charles Tindley learned to read is to start at the end. In the slot machine game of life, Tindley pulled the lever and—*chook, chook, ka-chook*—came up with triple sevens. The jackpot he won resembles quite closely the dreams that young people today on Delmarva—heck, young people all over the country and the world—have for their lives.

• He became a famous musician, helping to invent an entirely new genre, gospel music. He is a giant in the history of that field for lots of reasons. One example: He wrote the source hymn that morphed into the civil rights anthem, "We Shall Overcome."

• He became a force for good in the world. As a preacher he built one of the country's largest congregations. With 13,000 believers in his corner, Tindley helped tens of thousands of poor people. He fought the good fight against segregation and racism. Still standing in Philadelphia today is Tindley Temple, a majestic monument to his accomplishments.

• He became the equivalent in his day of a bigtime social media influencer—his words reprinted in newspapers, his sermons broadcast on the radio, his life advice going viral in pre-internet fashion.

'I Was No Stranger to Kicks and Blows'
Life usually doesn't work like a slot machine. Charles Tindley had to earn his jackpot. One of the many things that makes his story incredible is the way he started, showing great courage at an impossibly young age while facing odds that seem insurmountable.

He was born to poor black parents late in slavery times, near Berlin, in Worcester County, Md. His mother died when he was a toddler. His grief-stricken father struggled to make ends meet. Charles had to fend for himself at a young age to a degree that seems unimaginable today.

When I was only nine or ten years old I was required to do almost as much work as a man. I had to patch my own rough clothing and wash my one tow shirt in a tub of cold water and ashes, and then stand in the sun until it dried.

Starting when Charles was about eight, his cash-strapped father "hired out" his son in temporary rental arrangements that had Charles toiling at this farm, that farm, and then another farm. These weren't nine-to-five gigs. They were closer to full servitude. The boy would often live with the strangers on those farms full time, 24/7. Years later, while delivering sermons, Tindley would drop hints about how bad things got.

I was no stranger to kicks and blows.

Some of the people with whom I lived were very cruel. Many cold nights I had to sleep [outside] in fence corners and cover myself with leaves.

The Temptation of Forbidden Fruit

The first key moment in Charles Tindley's journey toward earning his jackpot touches on an oddity of slavery times. In written memoirs and oral histories, enslaved men and women sometimes share early childhood memories of close friendships formed with the white kids of their owners. Such pals were allowed to waltz innocently across the color line, playing games together and going on adventures. The relationships wouldn't last, of course. The friends would go separate ways as they aged into the prescribed roles of slavery society.

Something like this seems to have happened to Charles Tindley during those child-labor stretches on local farms. He and a white boy became friends. We don't know who that kid was, but Tindley recalled later how that friend shared with him basic facts about the letters of the alphabet and how they fit together.

[He] showed me such words as "dog," "man," [and] "boy."

Most blacks on the Eastern Shore during the 1860s were illiterate, and most whites preferred to keep it that way. This snippet of reading was forbidden-fruit stuff, but Charles loved the taste of that fruit. When that white-boy friend disappeared from his life, Charles had a problem. He didn't own any books. Nor could he get his hands on any. He found a solution in ... discarded trash.

My only reading [material] was bits of newspaper which I picked up on the roadside and hid in my bosom; for I had no pockets.

Tindley would pick up those scraps of paper whenever he could. After a long day of work on one or another of those "hired out" farms, he would wait until everyone was asleep and then lay flat and still, hoping no one would discover what he was up to. He'd light a little piece of long-burning "pine knot" wood. He'd reach down his shirt to pull out a rumpled bit of newspaper and commence studying.

I would mark with fire coals all of the words I could make out.

Slowly but surely, scrap by scrap, pine knot by pine knot, Charles taught himself to cobble together new and bigger words. Eventually he gained a sense for how those words fit into sentences and what those sentences meant.

I continued this way, and without any teacher, until I could read the Bible almost without stopping to spell the words.

Amazing to think about, no? But it reaches beyond amazing and enters miraculous territory when viewed in the context of what that boy would accomplish in life. He'd become a wordsmith for the ages, composing sermons and song lyrics that are still striking chords in human hearts nearly a century after his death.

'All the People Were Watching … the Boy with the Bare Feet'
Reading is what led young Charles into a public spotlight for the first time. The story of that Sunday begins like most of his other days, with a run of physical labor—in this case, driving cattle to pasture. Then, for reasons Tindley would later describe as a mystery even to himself, the idea popped into his head that he ought

to go to church. This doesn't seem to have been a routine thing up to this point in his young life, but he followed that whim, going AWOL from his labors.

The church was five miles away. He had no shoes. After the long walk and all that cattle driving, his clothes weren't exactly in Sunday-best shape. He did what he could, stopping to wash his filthy bare feet in a ditch and drying them off with leaves.

I ... reached the church in the middle of the afternoon, in time for Sunday school.

Feeling self-conscious about his disheveled appearance, Charles tried to lay low in the "gallery" of the church. But then came a call from the pulpit, the preacher inviting boys and girls who could read the Bible to come up front and show off their skills. Adding to the pressure: Lots of older white people were in that church.

One big lump after another rose in my throat.

But he *could* read the Bible! Why *shouldn't* he stand up? Steeling up his courage, Charles stepped from his gallery hiding place.

Many years later while delivering a sermon, Tindley would say that some of the white worshippers hissed and cleared their throats, trying to discourage the barefoot black boy from continuing his brave march toward the front of the church.

The minister that Sunday seems to have been an out-of-town guest of some sort. Perhaps as a newcomer that preacher didn't understand how those white folks felt and what he was supposed to do about it. Or perhaps, as one of Tindley's children would later speculate, he was simply "a true ambassador of the

Lord" welcoming this surprise of a boy.

Once up front, Charles waited his turn. The minister handed him a Bible, asking him to read John 4:14. Could everyone hear the nerves in his voice?

But whoever drinks of the water that I will give him will never be thirsty again.

Charles made his way back to his gallery hiding place.

All the people were watching and talking about the boy with the bare feet.

Charles Tindley's 'Indomitable Resolution'

Uncertainties abound. We don't know how old Tindley was. We don't know what church this was. An exhibit at the Calvin B. Taylor House Museum in Berlin speculates that the incident might have happened at Stevenson Methodist Episcopal Church, a congregation that still gathers today on that town's Main Street. What we know for sure is that Tindley would look back on that brave, barefoot march as a transformational experience.

From that moment my ambition to be educated knew no bounds.

I went back to my lodgings with an indomitable resolution to become all that God had put me in this world to be. ... I milked the cows that night with music in my ears and heart. My heart was strangely warmed, and the world was never the same to me.

And so he was off and running toward that slot-machine jackpot of a life.

31 EQUANIMITY
THE LIFESAVING SAINTS OF SMITH ISLAND, VIRGINIA

I wish I could have tagged along on Spady family vacations in the early 1900s. Every summer that clan would sail down toward the mouth of the Chesapeake Bay and dock on to Smith Island, Va. There they would enjoy the hospitality of a relative named George Hitchens. Later in life Elizabeth Spady Nottingham wrote up a few memories of those childhood trips. Kids frolicked through long days of splashing in the sea, exploring shipwrecks, hunting for crabs, and climbing up to the top of the Smith Island Lighthouse.

Then, come nightfall, they would sit back under the stars, exhausted. That's when their host would pay a visit.

Captain Hitchens would often come out at night, with his long-stemmed corncob pipe, and sit with us beside the ramp which the boats would slide down as they went to rescue someone. He would tell us tales of rescues he and his men had made.

Sailing 'Into the Jaws of Death'
George Hitchens led the U.S. Life Saving Service crew on Smith

Island for more than 30 years, between 1881 and 1915. Perhaps he regaled the Spady kids with the tale of New Year's Day, 1893, when the schooner *Edith Berwind* ran aground in thick fog and wild seas. Waves swamped the boat. In a desperate bid to survive crew members climbed up into the ship's rigging and lashed themselves in place.

They spent the whole night hanging up there. One of the seven men gave up and fell into the sea. Daylight put a miraculous sight before the survivors—a lifesaving boat, six men rowing furiously through stormy seas. These "surfmen" had been fighting waves for six miles by that point. George Hitchens stood at the stern, sculling. From a U.S. Lighthouse Service summary of that rescue:

At frequent intervals the waves half-filled the [lifesavers'] boat. ... Two oars were snapped in twain [along the way], but new ones instantly replaced them.

All six of those men survived. Later, the *Berwind*'s captain, R.W. McBride, would write:

I have not the ability [and] neither can I gather the words to speak of Captain Hitchens and his natural kindness toward wrecked people.

Actually, McBride did manage to come up with a powerful bit of prose:

To save us these men walked right into the jaws of death.

The Crew That Just Wouldn't Listen
There's one story in particular I'd have loved to have heard Hitchens tell. Another dreadful winter night: Jan. 8, 1883. The facts of the case are fascinating enough, but it's the emotions I'm really curious about.

The phrase "duty calls" seems a straightforward thing, driving first responders then and now to leap into action with danger in the air and lives on the line. But what if those lives belong to guys who behaved like idiots? How does "duty calls" feel when it means risking your life for guys who maybe kinda sorta don't deserve saving? How do you keep your eyes on the prize, maintain your equanimity while under incredible duress?

The *Albert Dailey* was on her way from Baltimore to New England when she ran aground in a thick fog and stormy seas. She was stranded 250 yards from the shore of Smith Island, but three miles from the life-saving station. The fog was so thick that patrolling surfmen couldn't see the ship. Hours passed. The mist finally lifted a bit around midnight.

Hitchens and his lifesavers pushed a carriage loaded with a 3,000-pound surfboat over three miles of undulating sands and tall grasses. They rowed out into furious waves, but the fog had thickened again. They couldn't find the *Albert Dailey*.

They returned to shore, caught their breath, and tried again. Success! By 4am, everyone was safe, healthy, and ashore. Case closed!

'They Laughed at His Fears'
Or not. The weather improved. In the morning the captain and crew of the *Dailey* asked to go see their ship, hoping it could be saved or salvaged. Hitchens obliged, his men rowing them out. A team from the Cobb Wrecking Company was already on board.

"Shipwreckers" were a thing back then. These private entrepreneurs made their living by getting grounded vessels back afloat or, in the case of total wrecks, salvaging as much cargo as they could.

The wreckers thought they could get the *Dailey* afloat again. The two parties cut a deal on the spot over the wreckers' fee. Some *Dailey* crew members decided to stay aboard and help the wreckers.

In the midst of this back-and-forth discussion, it started snowing. Hitchens had a bad, bad feeling. The *Evening Herald* newspaper in Carbondale, Penn.:

Keeper Hitchens entreated the sailors and wreckers to go ashore with him again in the lifeboat. But they laughed at his fears and declared that the wrecking company's surfboat, which was moored alongside, would carry them safely ashore in case of need.

Hitchens didn't buy it. He had his crew leave the life-saving boat on that beach, three miles from the station, just in case. He made sure the guys left on board knew the right way to signal they were in trouble. He told them to be ready with a foghorn, as lifesavers might need that sound to help find the vessel while rowing through fog and/or darkness.

Then Hitchens and his lifesavers headed back to the station. There is no way of knowing if—or how many—curse words might have filled the air along the way. By now you've guessed what happens. Snow gets heavier. Winds rise to gale force.

The sea was lashed into mountainous waves.

Remember the surfboat that made the wreckers feel oh-so-confident? Swept out to sea. Everything happened so fast aboard the *Albert Dailey* that no one had time to signal the lifesavers. Nine men scrambled up into the rigging.

The Calm in the Storm

Déjà vu all over again. Patrolling surfmen couldn't see the wreck through the fog. They didn't learn the *Dailey* was in trouble until one patrolman stumbled into wrecked bits of hatches and spars that had washed ashore. There is no way of knowing if—or how many—curse words filled the air when Hitchens and his team got the news.

I poked around some but didn't find very many details about the kind of man George Hitchens was. At least two visitors who wrote about their visits to Smith Island used the same adjective: *genial.*

A brief tidbit in the *Norfolk Virginian* newspaper about a hunting expedition described Hitchens as "the finest shot in the lower part" of Northampton County. My thought upon seeing that: You don't become an expert shot without knowing how to master your breath, calm your nerves, and concentrate fully on the target.

More evidence along these lines: Hitchens was an accomplished naturalist, always on the lookout for rare birds, bugs, and mammals. He made frequent contributions to the collection in what we know today as the Smithsonian Museum of Natural History. He discovered a new-to-science subspecies of cottontail, *Sylvilagus floridanus hitchensi*, informally known as the "Hitchens cottontail." Native to Smith and Fisherman's islands, it's now believed to be extinct.

'The Men Bent to It Cheerfully'

Hitchens would need to call on his reserves of calm and mindful attention during that deja-vu second night of the *Dailey* wreck. He had his team break out the life-saving "Lyle Gun," used to shoot rope lines out to a wreck so that stranded sailors could glide to safety in zip-line fashion. Alas, this meant another three-mile slog pushing a cart loaded with heavy equipment.

The wind and sleet blew dead in the faces of the men, the snow was over a foot deep and the beach sand mushy from the soaking tides which rolled over it. ... The task of hauling the cart and its load was almost beyond human strength, yet the men bent to it cheerfully.

Really, *cheerfully*?

Once at the beach the surfmen set off signal flares. They wanted the stranded sailors to know help was on the way if they could hang on just a little bit longer. Then it was back to rowing through pitch blackness, just like the previous night.

There was no light on the vessel, no sound, no foghorn signal as agreed upon.... [T]hey simply beat about in the dark at the mercy of the waves.

The danger didn't just come from heavy seas. The *Albert Dailey* was breaking apart, and pieces of its "plunging wreckage" threatened at nearly every pull at the oars to "send the boat and its brave crew to the bottom."

Again with déjà vu: They couldn't find the schooner in the dark and fog. They rowed back ashore to wait for dawn. Morning

262

light showed eight men lashed up in the rigging.

The spectacle kindled anew the valor of the exhausted and half-frozen surfmen.

The seas were too rough for rowing, so Hitchens's team broke out that Lyle gun. The first shot was a clean hit, line landing on the boat. None of the eight men made a move toward it. A second shot hit the mark, too. Again, no movement. Were the men up there too frozen to move, too close to dead? It was approaching noontime when Hitchens decided to try rowing again.

Keeper Hitchens and his men, though they had been out on the beach all night in the terrible storm without fire or food, drenched to the skin from their first effort to board the vessel, and keeping their feet from freezing only by wading in the salt water of the sea, yet rushed with alacrity to their duty.

How bad a shape were they in?

Their clothes, frozen upon them for many hours, literally cracked as they bent to the oars.

It took several tries to "clear the breakers" and get away from the shore. They rowed like heck, but current and waves blew them off course, away from the ship. They returned to shore. Brief catching of breath, then back at it. This time, they got close enough for a surfman to grab hold of the line that had been shot out of the Lyle gun.

But the sea was running so high that [the line] was snatched from the hand of the man who held it and again they were driven ashore.

Brief catching of breath, then back at it. The surfmen reached the *Dailey* on their third try. They managed to get four sailors loaded up before a wave swept the surfboat away from the schooner. Back to shore. Unloading unconscious bodies. Brief catching of breath, then back at it.

Cold, hunger, exhaustion, sleepiness are forgotten and the long hours of past toil seem but a moment to those men, now thrilled with the excitement of rescue.

They got the other four. A ninth man had fallen from the rigging in the night. One of the eight rescues would die on the beach that morning. Seven wreckers and sailors would survive.

Making a Case for Sainthood
Five hours passed before the first of them regained consciousness. Five days passed before they were stable enough to leave Smith Island.

As incredible as this rescue was, the thing I found most re-markable is what happened during that five-day recovery window. That Pennsylvania newspaper says that Hitchens and his men did their jobs in those days as if nothing unusual had happened, as if those men had not rejected good advice, acted irresponsibly, and put their lives and the lives of every man in the lifesaving crew at risk.

[Hitchens and his men] were not the kind to cry, "We told you so."

264

If that is true, I would hereby like to nominate George Hitchens and his crew for sainthood.

32 COMMUNITY
SHOULD YOU HATE THESE DO-GOODER DELAWARE WOMEN?

Delaware was abuzz with political contention in the spring of 1920. A civic debate that had roiled the nation for decades was nearing its crescendo. Now the state legislature was about to vote on the proposed 19th Amendment.

Should women have the right to vote?

Let's meet two of the women who played key roles in that debate. First, Emily Bissell. She launched the first-ever free kindergarten in Delaware. She worked to protect kids from abusive child-labor practices. She helped start a nonprofit called The West End Neighborhood House to help immigrants learn English, get jobs, and find housing. (That place is still going, with a broader mission of helping all types of Delaware families in need with education, entrepreneurship, emergency assistance, and more.)

Bissell borrowed a concept pioneered in Europe and launched this country's first-ever Christmas Seals campaign. That initiative saved a tuberculosis facility from financial woes. Activists in other states followed her lead, and that's how we ended up with our modern Christmas Seals, putting millions every year in the coffers of the American Lung Association.

Mary Thompson got into do-goodering after watching a new railroad line come through her New Castle County neighborhood and destroy a pond where kids loved to swim and skate. She helped launch the West End Athletic Club to give those kids a new and healthy playtime environment. The club eventually became a hub for social-reform-minded women chasing all kinds of other goals. Many good works sprouted from that West End seed.

Thompson and Bissell worked together to launch the Delaware Chapter of the American Red Cross. After Thompson and her husband bought a home in Rehoboth Beach she led the first-ever beautification campaign on that town's main drag, planting a gazillion flowers. She was an ace fundraiser for Beebe Hospital in Sussex County as well as for the National Association for the Prevention of Infant Paralysis.

She even declared war on the bane of Rehoboth existence, mosquitoes. People laughed at first, dismissing her as "The Mosquito Lady," but Thompson got the last laugh when she succeeded in convincing Delaware politicians to send a small army of workers from the Civilian Conservation Corps to focus on mosquito abatement.

Bottom line: We're talking about two smart, capable, and caring community leaders. Who wouldn't want the likes of Emily Bissell and Mary Thompson in their communities?

Oh, one other thing: Bissell and Thompson fought tooth and nail *against* the 19th Amendment. To make matters worse: They won the political debate. Delaware legislators rejected the amendment.

Good God, What Were They Thinking?
A confession. Before doing research on this, I failed miserably in trying to come up with an acceptable answer to that what-were-

they-thinking question. The only things I had as possibilities were insulting generalizations.

• These women were stupid.

• These women were brainwashed by a sexist, patriarchal society.

• These women were sheep, following orders from rich husbands and/or backwards-thinking preachers.

But that couldn't be. Mary Thompson and Emily Bissell accomplished so much! They helped so many people! There's a concept historians go back and forth about called *presentism*. That's the bad habit we often fall into of looking at the past through the lens of our present-day view. It's a lazy way of thinking that ignores how people in days gone by were living in radically different circumstances and coming at problems with different values. As the novelist L.P. Hartley famously put it,

The past is a foreign country; they do things differently there.

Let's try and get past this 19th Amendment presentism, shall we? Let's try to be fair to Thompson and Bissell, by stepping into their shoes and seeing the world through their eyes. First step in that direction, a quote from Mary Thompson:

It's not that I feel women cannot vote or are not of mental equality with our men folks.

Why, then, shouldn't they be able to vote? Bissell and Thompson built their most powerful argument around their own success stories as community leaders. They argued that the reason women like themselves were able to accomplish so much in civic do-goodering was precisely because women did *not* have the right to vote.

The best way to think about this is to consider how we regard religious organizations in our modern times. Churches get tax-free status as nonprofits, but that comes with some expectations. Churches should steer clear of partisan politics. They can't endorse candidates. They shouldn't fundraise for blatantly political causes.

That doesn't mean they can't do good works. They can feed the hungry and house the homeless. But in doing so, they are supposed to act from elevated motives, driven by faith and charity. They are supposed to be unsullied by the money-grubbing, vote-begging, power-hungry stuff of politics.

That's how Thompson and Bissell viewed the proper role of women in civic affairs. The brand of do-goodering they practiced was a maternal affair, not a political one. They strove to serve as loving caretakers to all of God's children in the way they cared for their own offspring. Their causes were pure, not political. Emily Bissell:

When the women of this state came to the Legislators [with a cause], the legislators knew we had no ulterior motive. They could act with a clear conscience, never asking "will she vote for me? Or will she not?"

If women got the vote, that would all change. The vote would knock women reformers off their pedestal, sending them into smoke-filled backrooms with all the other grubby interest groups—lobbyists, union bosses, corporate bigwigs, and the like.

They would go down in status, not up.

Forget the vote. Keep women pure. Let their maternal instincts rise above the civic fray. Then sit back and watch them accomplish great things.

Are You Convinced?

Me neither. But still: That's not the argument I expected. It's certainly not dumb. Nor is it the product of brainwashing. It comes from a place of generosity, a desire to be in the best position to lift up neighbors in need.

I have a caveat. Truth be told, I cherry-picked their best argument. Bissell and Thompson had some other debating points that come across as pretty lame. They wanted women to remain in their proper social place (keeping house, raising children), while men stay in theirs (at the workplace, managing civic affairs). But as lame as that sounds, it probably sounded quite different back in the "foreign country" of 1920, when the notion of women entering male workplaces still ranked as a pretty new, untested, and controversial phenomenon.

One other thing. I'm sad to report that Bissell and Thompson succumbed to temptation during that hotly contested campaign of 1920 and demonized some of their opponents. They dismissed suffragettes as a brand of pre-hippy, free-love floozies. They had unkind and arguably racist things to say about the impact "uneducated" black women might have on elections.

But guess what? The other side had lots of mean and hurtful things to say about Bissell and Thompson, too. Do you see what's funny about this ugliness? It kinda sorta proves the point Bissell and Thompson were trying to make in their best argument. Once they stepped down from a motherly pedestal and walked on the muddy turf of partisan politics, they ended up slinging mud and flinging insults.

They might as well have said, "We told you so."

Thank You, Ladies!

I'm glad women have the right to vote. I'm also grateful for the way Mary Thompson and Emily Bissell pop into my mind now and again. This happens when I find myself thinking bad thoughts about the motives and intelligence of people I disagree with.

The story of these two anti-suffragettes gives me pause. What don't I know about the lives of people I disagree with? Do they dole out food at soup kitchens? Do they get down and dirty on beach clean-up day? Do they tutor kids after school? Do they pay hospice visits to dying neighbors? What do I really know about where they're coming from or what kind of lives they lead?

That's usually enough to quell the bitter outrage and bring me back to my senses. Thank you, ladies!

33 COMMUNITY
PAST FORWARD IN CHINCOTEAGUE, 2023

I'm thinking I should close this book with a storybook tale. Something warm and fuzzy. You know, odds stacked against little guys, community in crisis. Friends step up. Strangers pitch in. Everything comes together. Curtain falls, cheers rise.

Another thought: I should close by bringing the theme into the present, showing how the generous, can-do spirit that so often characterized Delmarva in days gone by is still alive and kicking, how people on the peninsula are still writing inspiring tales of courage, kindness, and community. That would bring things full circle with a happy take on the famous William Faulkner quote:

The past is never dead. It's not even past.

Only one problem: The crickets.

That's the sound—or lack thereof—that greeted a woman on Chincoteague Island, Va. when she raised the alarm, warning that a cherished piece of island history was at risk of disappearing forever. The silence raises an issue that's on a lot of Delmarva minds these days. Yeah, we like progress. Progress is good. Most of the time. But then there's the Counting Crows brand of progress. Sing along:

Don't it always seem to go
That you don't know what you got 'til it's gone?
They paved paradise and put up a parking lot.

Is it even possible anymore to bring people together and say, "Sorry, not this time, not this place?"

The Nesting Dolls of Chincoteague
Let's set the stage. The history of that barrier island off the upper Eastern Shore of Virginia is thick with memorable stories on myriad themes, but one tugs more insistently on the heartstrings of Chincoteague lovers than all the others. That would be the ponies, of course.

Perhaps you've visited the island and snapped pictures of those chubby, diminutive horses roaming free on nearby Assateague Island. You've almost certainly heard of them. Misty of Chincoteague. Her foal, Stormy. The island's midsummer pony swim and auction is known around the world as a gloriously idiosyncratic tribute to a one-of-a-kind local tradition.

The history of those ponies unfolds in a whole run of tales, piled up one atop another like a collection of nesting dolls. In the beginning, shrouded deep in the mists of the past, lies a mystery. Where did the ponies come from? Did they swim ashore from the wreck of a Spanish galleon? Did dastardly pirates abandon them? The truth is probably more prosaic, with run-of-the-mill European settlers parking horses out on Assateague Island to graze sometime in the 1600s.

Going with the 'Flow'
But even in the prosaic version things take a storybook turn.
Have you seen the Oscar-winning movie "Flow," which follows a
motley collection of animated animals as they struggle against the
odds to survive in a strange, frightening new environment brought
on by a humongous flood?

The ponies endured a version of that. Left alone on the
island, they turned *feral*. That's a technical word ecologists use to
describe once-domesticated animals that revert back to living in
the wild. The transition must have been a nightmarish ordeal. No
barns or caretakers in sight. Floods, hurricanes, fires. The biggest
challenge was finding food in a landscape full of unappetizing,
salt-drenched grasses with scant nutritional value.

That lousy diet explains how—over the course of who
knows how many generations—a bunch of normal-sized horses
shrunk to a breed that in adulthood reaches pony size and that's it.
Somehow the ponies figured out that they needed to compensate
for all the extra salt going into their bellies by drinking twice as
much water as normal horses. That's why they look bloated and
chubby. Think about this feral business the next time you're out
on Assateague snapping pictures: The reason those ponies are
so adorably short and rotund is because they are tough-as-nails
survivors.

Pony Parties Across the Centuries
Another nesting doll, also set in the misty past. As I'm writing
this in 2025, Chincoteague is gearing up to celebrate the 100th
anniversary of that world-famous pony swim and auction. A
century is a long time, but the tradition of throwing pony parties
goes back much further. In *Once Upon an Island: The History of
Chincoteague*, historian Kirk Mariner guesstimates that the tradi-

tion is more than three centuries old, dating to the late 1600s or early 1700s.

The earliest written reference to a pony party comes in a magazine piece from 1835, by which point the party already ranked as an "ancient" tradition. The event had a functional purpose--ranching routines of branding, gelding, and buying and selling. But it was also an excuse to party.

The adjoining islands were literally emptied of their ... frolic-loving inhabitants, and the [mainland of the] peninsula ... contributed to swell the crowd. ... [The penning was] a scene of no ordinary revel, [an occasion of] unrivalled noise, uproar, and excitement.

Mariner dug up hints that things got even rowdier as time went on.

[During the mid-1800s] the festivities ... were punctuated with such heavy drinking and riotous revelry that the womenfolk stayed away from it, except to prepare the great quantities of food that the menfolk consumed.

After the Fire
Another nesting doll, this one with a touch of myth about it—phoenix rising from the ashes. The devastating fire that tore through downtown Chincoteague in September 1920 destroyed a dozen buildings and damaged many others. More blazes flared up in the years that followed—the island got stuck in a rut of bad fire luck. It became clear that it was time to create a state-of-the-art fire company, but there was a problem. There wasn't any money for that—not from the government and not in the private sector.

A fledgling Chincoteague Volunteer Fire Company formed anyway, then won permission in 1925 to put on a fundraising carnival during the pony-penning party. Someone got the bright idea to sell a few ponies in an auction.

Their timing was impeccable. With the rise of the automobile and the construction of a causeway linking the island to the mainland, it was now much easier to get to Chincoteague. Tourists flocked to the pony swim and auction in unprecedented numbers. In 1937 the crowd was estimated at 25,000. That's 10 times the number of people who lived on the island.

A Storybook Affair

In 1946 the throng of tourists at pony penning included a writer named Marguerite Henry. She visited a ranch on the southeast side of the island and met owners Clarence and Ida Beebe. She fell head over heels for a newborn foal. She bought that pony, christened her Misty, and had her shipped up to her home in Illinois.

Like most every other visitor to Chincoteague through the centuries, Henry was entranced by the beauty, tradition, culture, and hospitality of the place. It set her imagination on fire. Her 1947 children's book *Misty of Chincoteague* became a megahit, capturing the minds of horse-addled children around the country in the same manner as a later generation of wizard-addled kids would fall for Harry Potter. There would be four Misty books in a series, each a big hit. Hollywood made a Misty movie in 1961. Tourism skyrocketed. Here is Cindy Faith, a former director of the Museum of Chincoteague Island:

By putting us on a national stage like that, Marguerite Henry changed everything on the island.

276

A Stormy Affair

One last nesting doll, this one perched in the midst of catastrophe. Misty lived a celebrity life up in Illinois. Buses of schoolchildren and Girl Scout troops visited her. She made a VIP appearance at a convention of librarians. When Misty got to a certain age Marguerite Henry shipped her back to the Beebe ranch on Chincoteague. Fingers crossed: She wanted Misty to start a family.

Success! Phantom Wings was born in 1960. Wisp O'Mist arrived in 1961.

Then, disaster.

Misty was pregnant with her third foal when the hellacious Ash Wednesday storm hit in March 1962. The deluge lasted three long days and stretched across five high tides. More than 90 percent of Chincoteague Island flooded. The water ran six feet deep downtown on Main Street. The island's chicken industry was decimated, an estimated 350,000 birds dying. Ponies suffered horribly, with more than 100 deaths.

Lots of the island's humans evacuated, including the generation of Beebes then in charge at the ranch, Ralph and Jeanette. Before fleeing, they moved pregnant Misty into the kitchen of their small home. As news of the flood spread children across the country went apoplectic with worry. The Associated Press reported phones ringing off the hook with youngsters on the verge of tears, begging to know if Misty was still alive. The *Washington Post* felt the need to run a story with this headline:

Misty of Chincoteague Reported Safe

Misty spent three days in the kitchen. Then she got evacuated, too, to nearby Pocomoke City, Md. where she gave birth to a foal named Stormy. Misty and Stormy went on tour, taking star turns in theaters and at school assemblies in a campaign to raise money to help the pony herd recover from the flood. Marguerite Henry didn't have to work very hard on the plot for her next best seller, *Stormy, Misty's Foal*.

The Beebe Ranch on the Brink

We're done with nesting dolls. It's time to move into more recent events. The storied Beebe ranch covered 100 acres in its early days. The property shrunk bit by bit over time, this piece split off to a relative through inheritance, that piece sold off in a time of financial need.

The Beebes have never been a wealthy family. Remember Jeanette, the ranch-running matriarch at the time Misty survived the storm of 1962 in the kitchen? She worked for many years as a cafeteria lady at the local high school. That former Museum of Chincoteague Island director, Cindy Faith:

Jeanette absolutely did not want the ranch to be sold. There were times when things were really tough and she had to think about selling, but she always figured out a way. Her attitude was, "We will scrimp and save and do whatever we need to do."

Still, the ranch had dwindled down to just 10 acres by 2023. The Beebe in charge at this point was Billy, one of Jeanette's children. He, too, did his best to honor the nesting-doll history of the ponies and share the ranch's part in those stories with visitors. He and Cindy Faith became close friends while working together on various tours and projects over the course of decades.

Billy found himself in a bind. Ailing, older family members needed financial support. There was only one possible source of funds. He had no choice but to sell the ranch. Still, he wanted to do it in the right way. He broke the news to Faith, hoping against hope that she and her husband, Nathan Sears, might buy the property, keeping it in hands sure to honor its history.

The Faiths looked long and hard at that possibility. They even signed a contract giving them first option to buy the place for $625,000. But as they dug into the details, the Faiths saw that it wasn't going to work. Even if they could swing the purchase price, they'd have to sell most of the land to finance much-needed rehab work on the house.

Real-estate developers would be circling soon. Once that purchase option ran out, the price on the ranch was going to go up—and probably by a lot.

The Crickets

The Faiths went into frantic brainstorming mode.

What if we took ourselves out of the equation? Who else might buy the property and treat it with the reverence it deserves?

Only one last resort made sense. Faith was still working then as director of the Museum of Chincoteague Island. One evening, without warning, she dropped this bomb on her board of directors, telling them the story of those top-secret negotiations with Billy Beebe and warning that the future of the ranch looked bleak. She closed with a question:

Do you think maybe the museum could buy the ranch?

Crickets.

Actually, that was exactly the correct response. Everybody in that room had a grasp on the museum's finances. Like most local history museums, the Museum of Chincoteague Island operates on a thin margin, raising enough every year through events and fundraising campaigns to cover operating expenses. Faith wasn't asking them to think about some pipe dream off in the future. She was telling them that saving the ranch meant raising $625,000 on a three-month deadline.

I have some relevant experience, having served as the director of two small nonprofits on Maryland's Eastern Shore in recent years. If someone had suggested to me a project that involved bringing in that kind of money on that kind of deadline, I might not have responded with crickets. Instead, I might have tossed around a few f-bombs, because the notion that we might hit such a target … that's insane!

The meeting ended on that cricket note. Everybody went home. Time for some deep breathing. When the board regathered, Jill Jesters was the first member to speak up:

If we don't try to do this, we will never forgive ourselves.

Another board member, Denise Bowden, couldn't get to the meeting in person. Her text came in at the very moment Jesters was urging the museum step out onto a Beebe limb.

We're stewards for this island, its history. We have to go for it.

The unanimous decision came in late March. The deadline on Faith's option to buy the ranch had been extended by this point to June 30. That Billy Beebe stuck with the $625,000 price tag was an act of generosity—he could have gotten more on the open market.

That tight deadline left no time to apply for grants or meet with fundraising consultants or hold navel-gazing focus groups to identify best practices. Instead, Faith and the museum team launched in a mad rush, throwing the project out before the public via a hurriedly composed press release and some desperate-sounding social media appeals.

One day passed. Two days. Three. Four. They got a lot of likes on Facebook, but the mail brought ... crickets.

On day five two checks arrived. They were decent-sized, $5,000 apiece. On the one hand the museum team felt like doing cartwheels. On the other they did some math: Hmm, that's 1.58 percent of the goal. They opted to cling to the power of positive thinking.

We decided that, ok, this must be a sign, a sign this is going to happen.

More mail came in. Most of it amounted to $10 dollars here, $20 there. The campaign was 10 days old when Faith sat down with a VIP acquaintance who had deep connections on Virginia's Eastern Shore and long experience fundraising for community causes. The message that VIP delivered was worse than the crickets. Here is how Faith remembers it:

I know your heart is in the right place, but this is an incredibly foolish idea. You're never going to make this kind of money. The largest amount of money ever raised on the Eastern Shore, for anything, is maybe a quarter of a million dollars. You're going to tap out before you get enough. The museum can't afford this. You're going to be humiliated. You're going to have to return this money. It's time to say, "Hey, we tried, but we can't do it." You should back out, now.

Faith talked it over with museum leaders. Everyone decided to cling tighter to the power of positive thinking.

We knew that maybe we were just being naïve. But we decided to say, "Sorry. We're gonna make this happen."

'Miracle After Miracle After Miracle'

It's true that there's only so much charitable money available in small communities. But those pony nesting dolls have an emotional reach that extends far beyond Accomack County, Va. This wasn't just a local cause. It touched the hearts of most everyone who'd ever visited Chincoteague, as well as most everyone who'd read *Misty of Chincoteague*. Newspaper and television editors from coast to coast understood that. Faith:

It's that kind of story, a heartwarming cause. People feel like there's so much negativity in the world. Editors and producers know that. They were like, "Hold on, here's a story that will make people feel good. We should share it."

That geography of media coverage became apparent in daily mail deliveries. One day, a gaggle of small donations from California. Hey, I guess somebody out there ran a story! A couple of days later, a batch from Massachusetts. Then Georgia. Or Texas. Opening the mail became a joy, especially on the day a donation arrived in a card adorned with a child's crayon drawing of a horse. That horse looked more like a skinny dinosaur, actually, but it was a beautiful dinosaur! The kids from a 4-H club in New Jersey signed it, first names only:

Ordinary Heroes of Old Delmarva

Desmond, Allison, Angela, Anna, Lela, Elin, Emma

An elderly woman on a fixed income called on the phone, over-come with emotion. She was thinking about taking out a personal loan to finance a donation and wanted to discuss the proper amount.

Absolutely not! No, no, no! Please! Do not take out a loan!

That woman scrounged up $50 and sent it in. A letter arrived from France, with a note in French and a check from a French bank. Donations came from Germany, too. People made jewelry, created pony products, and crafted quilts, then sold them online or at events, all proceeds earmarked for the Beebe ranch in honor of those pony nesting dolls. While recounting all this, Faith twice had to pause and wipe away tears.

Opening the mail every day, it's like "Wow, look at how much people love this place! How can we not do everything we can to make this happen?"

Some notes were deeply personal.

One woman wrote a letter telling us about the horrible childhood she had. Then a librarian at school gifted her a copy of Misty of Chincoteague. She knew her father wouldn't like the idea of her getting a gift like this, so she had to hide it. She would read it under her bed covers at night. And she said that she kind of materialized herself into the lives of the book's young heroes, Paul and Maureen. She fantasized that she was Maureen. That was her escape. She said the story kind of kept her alive, really, and gave

283

her something to dream about. She still re-reads the books, once a year.

The museum received an astounding 5,000 small and medium-sized donations, ranging between a few dollars and a few thousand. That brought in half the purchase price. Three big donors stepped up with the other half. Two were individuals, giving $100,000 apiece. The third was the Chincoteague Volunteer Fire Company, which held a special auction for the cause. That pony fetched a record price.

I mean, it was just miracle after miracle after miracle.

The miracles kept on coming, right up to the end. On June 29, one day before closing, Faith went public with news of the thrilling, against-all-odds victory. The campaign was within $5,000 of the $625,000 goal. The museum planned to go ahead with the purchase and cover that last bit by throwing a fundraising event down the road. Instead:

Within an hour a woman shows up at the museum with a check for $5,000.

Donations kept rolling in after the deadline. The generous folks who were too late to pitch in on the purchase were happy to switch their money over to the mountain of work still undone—rehabbing the ranch house, planning and fabricating exhibits, and so much more. The museum hired a local contractor to do one of those preliminary jobs. Faith discussed with that guy some things that needed doing down the road when money became available. She and her husband went on a weeklong vacation. They returned to find those other jobs completed, gratis.

Faith resigned as museum director. She then took on the job of creating and managing the new incarnation of the Beebe ranch. Who knows? Perhaps the work she does will rank someday as a nesting doll of its own.

Those Footprints from Days Gone By
I started this book talking about how we walk today in the footprints of Delmarva days gone by and how this book aimed to help us see the ways we can find inspiration for our modern-day challenges in those footprints. So it was quite fitting when Faith ended our conversation right on that that theme. She thinks often in the wake of the save-the-ranch campaign about Jeanette Beebe, the cafeteria lady who fought tooth and nail to hold on to her Beebe nesting doll and treat it in a way that did right by the community of Chincoteague Island and its history.

Yeah, I see Jeanette up there in heaven. She's looking down on all the people who pitched in, coming from so many different places. She's nodding her head. She's saying, "Would you look at that? They made it happen."

Afternotes
• The last Beebe in charge of the ranch, Billy, had planned to work closely with Cindy Faith and the Museum of Chincoteague Island team on building a bright new future for the property. Alas, he passed away in 2024.
• The Beebe Ranch opened to the public as a museum in the summer of 2025, just as this book was going to press. Best of luck to Cindy Faith and her team!

BOOK CLUB DISCUSSION GUIDE

Are you in a book club? Did you find the themes here striking and worthy of discussion? Did you find specific stories that fit the interests of your group? Would you like to review a discussion guide filled with potential topics and questions?
Find one at this link:
secretsoftheeasternshore.com/book-club-ordinary-heroes

Or email me and I'll send it to you:
SecretsoftheEasternShore@gmail.com

ABOUT SECRETS OF THE EASTERN SHORE

Thank you so much for spending time with this book!

The husband-and-wife duo of writer Jim Duffy and photographer Jill Jasuta created Secrets of the Eastern Shore to celebrate and share the joys of the Delmarva Peninsula in words, pictures, and products. The pair has lived near the Choptank River in Cambridge, Md. since 2004.

Duffy started out in newspaper journalism in his hometown of Chicago, then moved into magazine writing and book projects after moving east. Jasuta started as a newspaper writer, too, before transitioning into graphic design and photography. Both have won numerous awards for their work over the years. Visit the website SecretsoftheEasternShore.com to see what they've been up to lately. The site has an ever-changing array of interesting tales, stunning photos, and assorted travel tips, along with a line of products—books, photo prints, and Delmarva-themed greeting cards.

Month of Fundays!
You should subscribe to the Month of Fundays newsletter. It connects you at the beginning of each month with info on upcoming

events all over the Delmarva Peninsula.
Sign up on the website:
SecretsoftheEasternShore.com.
Or send an email and I'll sign you up manually:
SecretsoftheEasternShore@gmail.com

Delmarva Stories, Trips, Photographs, & More:
SecretsoftheEasternShore.com
Facebook.com/SecretsoftheEasternShore

Other Secrets of the Eastern Shore Books:
Eastern Shore Road Trips #1:
27 One-Day Adventures on Delmarva

Tubman Travels:
32 Underground Railroad Journeys on Delmarva

Eastern Shore Road Trips #2:
26 MORE One-Day Adventures on Delmarva

You Wouldn't Believe:
44 Strange and Wondrous Delmarva Tales

Shore Fun!
The Delmarva Wanderer's Guide

Bookstores, retail shops, and other purchase options:
SecretsoftheEasternShore.com/product-category/books

Feedback:
SecretsoftheEasternShore@gmail.com; 443.477.4490

ABOUT THE TEAM

Jim Duffy wrote the book. All errors are his and his alone. A co-founder of Secrets of the Eastern Shore, he has written six books (so far!) on travel, culture, and heritage in the Delmarva Peninsula. See what Duffy has been up to lately:
SecretsoftheEasternShore.com

Jill Jasuta designed the cover. A co-founder of Secrets of the Eastern Shore, she is a photographer, graphic designer, and writer. Check out her latest work:
Facebook.com/JillJasutaPhotography
Instagram.com/JillJasutaPhotography
SecretsoftheEasternShore.com/product-category/print

Paul Clipper designed the interior pages of the book. An award-winning newspaper writer and magazine publisher, he has written several books about the art, adventure, and history of dirt-bike riding. He is also an amateur luthier and makes guitars out of cigar boxes for fun. Search his author name at Amazon books for more.

We all thank you for spending a little time with our work. Here's hoping the stories in this book add some sparks of inspiration to your days.

www.ingramcontent.com/pod-product-compliance
Lightning Source LLC
Chambersburg PA
CBHW021219130626
46554CB00004B/1285